Battlers of the Barkly

The Family Saga of Eva Downs

1936-1960

Alf Chambers

To Aunt Vianney   Xmas '99

Hope you enjoy the read

Love Wes Sue Roz Lisa &
Amy.

Alf in action during a cutting competition. This was the very
first campdrafting competition at Brunette Downs in 1951.

First published in 1998 by
Central Queensland University Press
PO Box 1615
Rockhampton, Queensland 4700

National Library of Australia
Cataloguing-in-Publication entry:

 Alf Chambers
   Battlers of the Barkly

 ISBN: 1 875 998 446

 1. Chambers family. 2. Australia - Genealogy. I. Title

 929.20994

Edited by Bobbie Buchanan.

Designed and typeset by David Myers
in Times New Roman and Gaze Normal

Printed and bound by
Watson Ferguson & Co, Brisbane

The painting on the front cover is "Campfire" by Australian bush artist Rosemary Carson, nee Copeland. Rosemary is a self-taught artist whose work reflects her love and understanding of the bush where she has spent most of her life. Her works have been displayed in exhibitions in Sydney, Brisbane and Toowoomba and in country centres throughout Queensland.

Dedication

To the two most special women in my life - To my mother, Lucy, in recognition of the caring, love and devotion shown under very trying conditions. She followed her determined, pioneering husband without a thought for herself, undoubtedly through the prime years of her life.

To my dear wife, Shirley, for her love, encouragement, great faith and support in writing this book through a time when she was battling terminal illness.

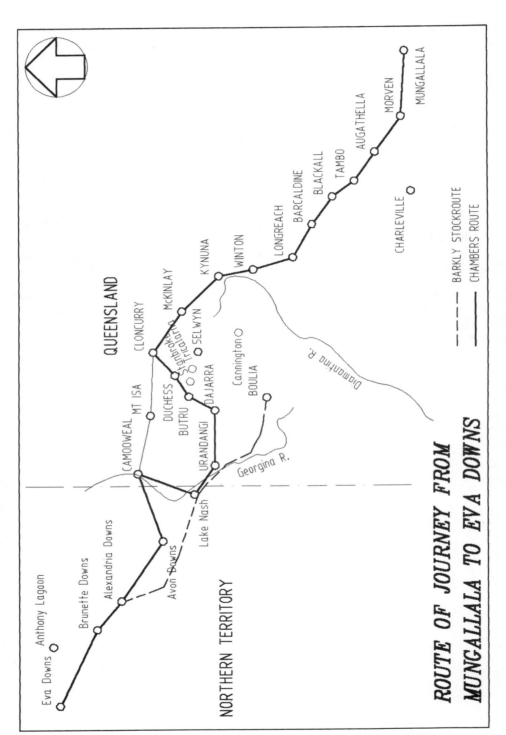

Map of journey from Mungallala to Eva Downs.

Contents

Part 1
Born to Battle

Part 2
The Battle for Eva Downs

Part 3
Triumph of the Battlers

Acknowledgements

First and foremost, I would like to thank my dear wife Shirley for her love and encouragement before her untimely ill health. I also greatly appreciate the many devoted hours my daughter Sue Presho has put in on her computer, recording what I have written.

I should also like to put on record my appreciation of the way in which Bobbie Buchanan has skillfully condensed my original manuscript whilst retaining my story style and description.

Thanks to Bruce Simpson, Marie Mahood and Professor David Myers for their sound advice and encouragement. Also Rosemary Carson (nee Copeland) for the wonderful painting for the cover, Bob Chambers and his daughter Jenny Hegarty for their wonderful illustrations of unphotographed events that happened through the years. Other people who have lent photos are Olive Price, Colin Chambers, Harry and Ruth Chambers, Stafford Burey, Reverend Fred McKay, Herb Cesari and Jamie Long.

I would like to thank colleagues in Local Government, Stan Wallace, Taroom A & P Association, Malcom McKosker, Ned Winter (Ned's Corner, Cecil City), James Walker Jnr, Terry Russell, Robert Adams and the multitude of others for their encouragement, support and assistance during the time it has taken me to put this story together.

Finally, I would like to express my gratitude to all my friends not mentioned above and hope that I have not hurt anyone's feelings by what I have written.

Foreword

I first met Sid Chambers in 1946 when Joe Dowling and I called in at 'Eva Downs'. Sid was a genuine character, a rugged individualist devoid of all pretence. What you saw was what you got with Sid. Few would have picked him for a station owner. The tough old pioneer must have made quite an impression on me, because I remember the incident as though it were yesterday.

Sid and his family had caused quite a stir when they first entered the Territory. A stockman seeing the cavalcade of horse-drawn vehicles and animals galloped back to camp and told his boss that a circus was passing by. If people were sceptical about the family's prospects, they were soon to be proved wrong. It is history now that in twenty four years Sid Chambers and his four sons transformed the vacant Eva block into one of the finest cattle stations in the Northern Territory. The story of the family's triumph over adversity makes fascinating reading; it is a story that should be an inspiration to us all.

I worked on 'Eva Downs' during one of the worst droughts in living memory. Sid had retired then, leaving the running of the property to the boys. Alf and his brothers were never armchair managers; they rolled up their sleeves and got stuck in. Anyone who kept up with them needed no rocking to sleep at night. We worked long hours, but it was always a team effort. I felt I was working with Alf and his brothers rather than for them. With the drought at its worst it was decided to move the cattle into the dried-up lake country. It was a virgin area, rich in blue bush, and excellent stock feed. Colin and I secured the new grazing land with new boundary fences. Bill put down new bores, while Alf had the job of building earth tanks with horse-drawn ploughs and scoops. As soon as Bill struck water, it was pumped into the partly completed tank. From then on it was a race to build the tank walls higher than the rising water level. On at least one occasion Alf and the horse team ended up in the drink. Finally Jack organised the moving of the cattle to the new area. By dint of enterprise and hard work the 'Eva Downs' herd was saved. Many neighbouring properties suffered disastrous stock losses. The friendships forged in those hard times have endured to this day.

Battlers of the Barkly is much more than a history of the Chambers family. Outback characters come alive in its pages and every chapter is enriched by the inclusion of humorous bush yarns and anecdotes; above all it is a book that portrays the real outback. Alf Chambers is a genuine bushman, a proud member of a pioneering family - Aussie battlers of the type that made this country great.

Bruce Simpson
Caboolture, Qld.

Introduction

In the 1930s conditions in the outback had changed little from the previous century. Big landholders occupied all the well-watered grasslands while large areas of poorly watered, but good grazing country lay idle. In the 1920s bores made it possible to run stock on this dry country and many small landholders wished to take up that challenge. The relationship between the big and small landholders was an uneasy one. No properties were fenced and herd management was often poor, resulting in many unbranded cattle. The large landholders were jealous of their cleanskins and suspicious of their new neighbours.

The Chambers' story encompasses a period of monumental change in the north. Motor vehicles had been introduced but there were no all weather roads, the pedal wireless was in its infancy and the aeroplane was just making its appearance. Few people realise that the Northern Territory was still being pioneered a mere 60 years ago. The second World War brought the 20th century to the Territory and a way of life disappeared forever along with the bagmen, the drovers, the travelling mailmen, the horse and cart and a multitude of eccentric bush characters.

During the 1930s, in the midst of a depression, Sid Chambers took up Eva Downs on the Barkly Tableland in the Northern Territory. Through sheer hard work and dedication the family defied the big landholders and succeeded in establishing a cattle station on an abandoned run. Several attempts had been made by others to develop the splendid grasslands but had failed through lack of water.

This is the story of Alf Chambers and his family, of a way of life, of a breed of Australians who have almost disappeared from the landscape they did so much to develop. It is a simple yet important record of pioneering and the everyday battles of small settlers to beat the isolation, the elements, the big landholders, government ineptitude, and the odds in general.

In recording his family's story Alf has preserved the unique history of latter day pioneering in the Territory. The credit is his and the privilege to have helped him is mine.

Bobbie Buchanan.

Portrait of Sid Chambers.

Sid and Lucy Chambers on their wedding day.

Part 1

Born to Battle

1.

From the Mallee Country to Queensland

Lucy's husband Sid, wanted the family to move to a new property he was establishing in the Northern Territory. She was reluctant to uproot the children and leave the security of her home, family and friends for an isolated and undeveloped outpost on the Barkly Tableland. Alf, her fourteen year old son, the third in a family of seven, had only had two years of formal schooling and she was particularly worried about his education. When she voiced her concerns to Sid, he impatiently replied, "I'll do that for him while he's looking up the rear of the horses all the way to the Northern Territory."

Sid found his wife's lack of enthusiasm for the new project irksome and being of a somewhat dictatorial nature he eventually issued an ultimatum, "You stay if you like but I'm taking all the children, no matter what happens!" As the youngest child was only three years old Lucy had no option but to accept defeat gracefully. She tried her hardest to provide care and comfort for all and prepared swags, camp gear, clothing chests, ports, tucker boxes and a small medical kit, for the arduous journey ahead.

Sid had sold his land near Mungallala in preparation for the move to 'Eva Downs', but Lucy refused to sell the small farm that he had bought in her name, preferring to lease it to a friend. This annoyed Sid, who claimed buying the property in Lucy's name was the worst day's work he ever did!

Once his authority was established on the domestic front, Sid set about his preparations. First he did a wheel-right's job on the three horse drawn vehicles he planned to haul north. Steel tyres were removed and placed in roaring boxtree bark fires to heat. Then, with the help of a crimping vice-like tool they were shrunk and before they had completely cooled, refitted on the wooden wheels so that they would fit tightly. Next he made all necessary repairs to the harness and rigged a framework above Lucy's little buggy, which was then covered with birkmyre weather-proof cloth to provide protection from the elements.

After the team horses were mustered, the horse breaking commenced. Even Jack and Alfie broke in a couple of youngsters bred from the kid's ponies. The rest were chain horses which were given a few days work scooping and dam repairing so that they were ready to be harnessed to the wagonette. Behind this was hitched a light dray, carrying some earth-scooping equipment, which Sid thought might be useful. Beneath the wagonette was slung a raw cowhide with netting around the sides, in which to cage the poultry. Upon it was a dismantled Meadowbank scoop, Sid's favourite type of earthmover, and a very heavy road plough. With such a heavy load to pull it was little wonder the team of five draught horses became leg-weary before they reached the Territory border.

While mustering the horses one day, Sid saw a small crawler tractor working on a dam. It was the first of its kind in the district but it failed to impress him. Like all died-in-the-wool teamsters, he was against machines and frequently claimed that they would never replace horses. But within ten years most team horses were redundant. Everyone who could afford a crawler tractor for earthmoving had one, with the exception of the Chambers who struggled on using horse teams until 1956.

By the end of the first week of February 1938, in the age of the motor car, the caravan of horse drawn vehicles, riders and loose horses lined up ready to start the long trek out west. Quite a number of relatives and friends gathered to wish them 'bon voyage'. Sid had harnessed the horses to the wagonette with two leaders out front and three wheelers behind. A freshly broken chain mare was on an outrigger beside the horse in the shafts with a quiet horse on the other side. When he jumped up to his seat the youngster kicked out at the wooden splash board beneath the driver's feet. Sid promptly gave her rear end a couple of stripes with the whip sending the team into a very fast trot down through the high netting gateway. They swung wildly around a sharp turn onto the dusty Morven road, which is now the Warrego Highway, where he kept them going for a mile or so to get the starch out of the young one. This made grand entertainment for some of the well wishers, who had ridden along to watch the show and say their final goodbyes.

In the fierce summer heat, Lucy, driving her double-seated buggy pulled by two horses and accompanied by four of her children, followed in her husband's wake. Bill, the eldest boy, was already in the Territory, while Jack and Alf brought up the rear of the cavalcade driving the twenty-eight spare horses. Colin aged twelve, the two girls, Olive aged eight and Daisy aged six and the toddler, Harry, rode with Lucy. Years later one of the onlookers remarked that there were children's heads sticking out all over Lucy's little chariot. Leaving home was a sad day for her. She didn't believe for a minute that the trip would be one long picnic, or anything like the story Sid told the children.

Sid was born the third eldest son in a family of ten children, seven boys and three girls. The Chambers hadn't been selected by the best British judges and shipped to Van Diemen's Land in chains, they were of British migrant stock and came out as free settlers. Sid's grandparents, Joseph Chambers, a twenty-five year old labourer and his wife, twenty-two year old Susannah (nee Smith) made application for passage to South Australia under the Wakefield Scheme. They had an infant daughter and son, both of whom appear to have died on the voyage aboard the ship 'Navarino' which arrived in Adelaide on 6th December, 1837. A third child was born soon after their arrival in the Colony.

Sid's father, Joseph, moved from the Barossa Valley to the Geelong area where he set up a dairy and married Eliza Jane Reynolds in 1870. They too raised ten children. Three girls, Alice, Lily and Effie, and seven boys, Charles, William, Sidney, Henry, Albert, Frank and Stephen. Sid was formally christened Joseph Sidney, and was born at Wychitella in 1878. Dark complexioned, like his mother, the legacy of a Spanish influence, he was inclined to be a rover. Perhaps he also inherited it from his father, who too was inclined to range far from home in search of the elusive metal, even as far afield as Gympie. Meanwhile Eliza remained in Victoria running the dairy while the boys tried to grow wheat. Joseph secured them a raw piece of scrub land in the northern Mallee around the Lake Bogga area, into which to pour their youthful energy. The youths spent a number of years of hard gut-busting slog, grubbing enormous Mallee root stumps. It was the only way of clearing land in those days and resulted in sweat, calluses and blisters. Although the wheat returned a small annual income, the boys soon became disenchanted because in spite of their hard work, yields were poor from the sandy soil.

Although old Joseph didn't strike it rich in the goldfields, he earned quite good money by turning his hand to cutting railway line sleepers from forest country, using crosscut saw and broadaxe. This venture was so lucrative he only returned home during the warmer months of the year and for a period at Christmas. He never put any money towards getting the wheat farm properly established and the sons became restless and started to leave.

Sid, Frank and Albert were all good teamsters and took work ploughing and earth dam building. Charlie won a contract loading wheat bags onto railway trucks and was ably assisted by his sisters, Ada and Lily. Sid and Bill, thinking themselves physically fit after their rough bush life thought they could handle loading wheat bags too. There was no such thing as a conveyor, the method was to toss a bag onto stout shoulders then walk up a gang plank with the load. Bill was astonished to find that when he was beginning to buckle at the knees at the end of the day, his two sisters were still going strong!

When Sid heard the stories of gold at Kalgoorlie in Western Australia he decided to save for his boat fare. However, by the time he paid his coach fare to Melbourne, and a couple of day's hotel tariff and bought a few much needed items of clothing there wasn't enough money for the ticket, so he sought to work his passage as a sailor. The ship's captain would not sign on crew for such a short trip so Sid signed on for Capetown and return to Perth. He liked the idea of seeing Capetown and thought the experience as a sailor wouldn't do him any harm. Once out at sea the ship struck bad weather on the Great Australian Bight and he wasn't sure if he would live to see Perth and decided there and then that he wasn't cut out for a seafaring life.

On board he struck up a friendship with a sheep grazier's son returning to Perth after holidaying in the Eastern States. When his new-found friend disembarked, he carried Sid's few possessions with him. After the ship had unloaded its cargo and pulled off about 300 yards to anchor overnight, Sid jumped ship and swam ashore. When the roll was called next morning, sailor Sidney Chambers was missing.

Almost immediately he found work in a brick yard. Here he learned that prospectors were leaving Kalgoorlie because of lack of water and outbreaks of typhoid and scarlet fever, so he changed his mind about prospecting. Word got to him that there was good roo-shooting upcountry so he bought a .38 calibre rifle and reloading gear to load his own ammunition. This was much cheaper than buying it. Lead, bought in rolled sheets, was first heated in a heavy pot over an open fire before being poured into a moulding tool. The moulding tool had a resizing hole into which the brass powder case was inserted to bring it back to size before reloading. Then a new firing cap was fitted and a measure of black gun powder poured in before a new lead projectile was fitted to the shell. The range of the firearm was about 70 to 120 yards and was a utility type, suitable for the job, but unlike the Martini Henry with its long barrel used more for big game hunting, not too heavy to carry.

The roo-shooting was a profitable enterprise for Sid so he set out to save for the purchase of horses, saddle and pack saddle and camp equipment to set himself up as a professional roo shooter. There was good skin-hunting around Bunbury so he took a job at a timber yard there and was joined by his brother Bill, who had been prospecting in Kalgoorlie. Disillusioned by the poor conditions at the diggings he decided to get out before it was too late.

The brothers worked as a team. Sid did the shooting while Bill shifted camp and pegged the skins. When roos were scarce they did contract work. They followed the occasional shed as blade shearers and also undertook to drain some swamp land, digging channels with shovels for several miles to allow water to escape so that pasture grass would grow. The job paid well but was very heavy work. As a result of his knowledge of this swamp country, Sid's services were sought by a surveyor looking for the best rail link through that low lying country. In order to feed his workers, one rail line construction contractor bought roo meat at five pence per pound. This made the roo shooting venture doubly attractive and they employed a man to do the extra work. Most of the new settlers thereabouts ate kangaroo meat. A couple of years later the Government restricted each property to two bodies per week because the roos were becoming so scarce.

Bill was the first brother to become a landholder when he bought a property called 'Craigmore' in the Bogup Brook area. Soon after Sid secured a piece of country nearby and erected a bark hut and horse paddock. By this stage their financial resources were exhausted and the roos were shot out, so they existed on possum meat. Bill thought this the poorest of diets and named Sid's place 'Poverty Point,' and it is still called that today.

Soon after buying their blocks the brothers became attracted to the local young ladies. Bill's romance flourished into matrimony. Sid helped his brother construct a very staunch, jarrah slab walled homestead for his wife and they remained there for some sixty odd years. For a time they continued to work together, Bill caring for the land while Sid went off contract horse-breaking, shearing and horse-dealing. Bill was never fond of horses but Sid was an above average horseman and trapped and broke in brumbies for sale.

The pair decided to get into wool growing and worked together clearing, developing and establishing their own sheep farms. The work wasn't as laborious as grubbing mallee stumps, but it was still hard. Though the area had a reliable winter rainfall the impoverished sandy soil required plenty of fertilizer to support good wool-producing sheep. Before subterranean clover was introduced, the country's carrying capacity was approximately one sheep to three or four acres. After the introduction of the clover this rate increased to five to seven sheep to the acre because it provided the soil with nitrogen.

Sid still went roo-shooting whenever there were any around. With a packhorse carrying his camp equipment, wire nail pegs, camp oven and waterproof tarpaulins to cover dried skins, he followed where the animals were thickest. One of his most prized possessions was a possum skin rug which he claimed was the warmest thing he ever slept in. With the addition of one aged blanket and a water proofed sheet to go both under and over his body he was able to sleep out in the coldest frosts and have more room on the packhorse for other camp gear. Sometimes in the winter months when the season was open, he also carried possum snares and Bill called at his camps once a week to collect the skins.

When Sid received the news that his mother was in poor health, he took a ship home to Victoria to visit her and had a much more enjoyable trip than previously. One day the sea was rough and the roll of the ship was upsetting the passengers. He had just had dinner and was priding himself on not feeling seasick when he came across an attractive lady clutching the railing and heaving ever so violently over the side. Walking over he gallantly offered to assist her back to her cabin but when she turned to face him she let a good measure go all over Sid! Instantly he was beside her at the rail feeding the fish, and forgot all about his offer to the lady who had to her make her own way back to her cabin.

After visiting his mother he continued his journey up to Queensland to see his brothers, Albert, Frank and Charles. He stayed for a while and became impressed with the twenty-three inch rainfall country. Although it wasn't anything like the rainfall in Western Australia it was a long way better than the Mallee. Most of all, there was good grass and even a crop of wheat could be grown without fertilizer, as a few local farmers were proving. Sid decided to buy 8,500 acres of land on the Dulbidilla Creek, over which Albert had held grazing rights. He called the property 'Lilypool' after the waterhole there.

Brother Albert was married with two children before he left Victoria. He set out alone on the wallaby. Riding a pushbike and carrying his swag and tucker bag he pedalled through New South Wales into Queensland looking for likely land to settle. His first choice was excellent belah scrub country near the town of Condamine. Unfortunately this was being threatened by prickly pear. Arsenic pentoxide was the only known method of destroying it then and Albert realised he couldn't work with it, so he chose to go on out to Mungallala. There he got a job as a teamster hauling logs to a saw mill and selected land about ten miles down the Mungallala Creek. He engaged a carpenter to build a house and set off by buggy to Victoria, to pick up his young wife and family.

The house was situated right by the creek so Albert called it 'Riverside'. Like the small settlers nearby he chose to grow wheat, and for the next few years they were blessed with favourable winter rain. Albert also went in for sheep, though he realised he would have the expense of erecting six foot dingo netting fences. To finance this scheme and for his own use he started breeding and breaking in heavy horses. Frank and Charlie Chambers also settled in the area. Charlie sold his farm in 'Ultima' in the Mallee and bought a property next door to Albert.

Frank, who was a tall man weighing fifteen stone, is said to have been a gay blade and quite light on his feet. One night, cutting a dash in his swallow tail suit he went along to a local dance, where he performed the Lancers with a very popular local lass. The romance was short-lived when he gave an energetic hop and one of his flying coat tails revealed a large kangaroo-skinning knife on his belt.

There were numerous tales of the brothers' wheelings and dealings, particularly when they put a mob of horses together to take to Victoria. Frank always had an eye out for a stylish hack and had bought a nice thoroughbred mare that he discovered bucked pretty well. Sid and Albert were at the stockyard when Frank put his big, knee-pad, rough-riding saddle on the mare which she promptly tried to buck off. Albert said, "I think you'd better let Sid ride her as he is the better rider."

"No, she's right. She's my mare, just tie the stirrup irons and I'll show you I can ride her," said Frank.

They blindfolded the mare while the stirrups were tied then gave Frank a leg up. Once in the saddle he reefed off the blindfold and she bucked around but he stuck to her. He then called for the gate to be opened and the mare took off bolting and bucking down the paddock. Sid said, "I think I should catch a horse to follow him."

Albert, always a great tea drinker, said, "No. We'll have a cup of tea."

Several times Sid said, "I think I should get my horse to follow him."

"Have another cup of tea!" was Albert's response.

After about the fourth cup, Frank came to the door with a great grin on his face and his saddle and bridle over his shoulder. He said, "The third fence stopped her. She fell over it and broke her neck!"

On a cold and frosty morning Frank was wearing a big army overcoat while he broke in a young chain horse in a small yard. He had a long head rope attached to it when the horse somehow broke the gate latch and took off with Frank in hot pursuit at the end of the rope. The young horse careered across the big yard, smashing the two top rails. Frank followed, hurdling the top-most remaining rail and the increasing pace of the horse forced him to take longer and longer strides. When he got to the ploughed ground he fell over but was still determined to hang on. As he was towed along on his chest and stomach, somewhat like a plough, the weeds built up too high to see over. In real Salt Bush Bill fashion, he then let go.

In all, the brothers made three trips to Victoria with mobs of 300 — 500 jointly owned horses for sale. After the first trip Sid returned to the West and sold his property to Bill. Combined the properties would only support one family but the good winter rainfall and later the introduction of the subterranean clover changed that.

Sid returned to Melbourne just in time for the show and he bought a champion Clydesdale stallion —an enormous animal. It was shipped to Brisbane and Sid followed by train, arriving at the same time as the ship. Wanting to view the horse to make sure it was O.K. before railing it out to Mungallala he approached Dalgety's, the agents. They had been told that Sid had a long black beard but now he was clean-shaven, so they refused to let him near the horse. Finally a bank manager officially identified him.

Lucy's sisters Mary and Clara.

Lifelike models of cattle made by Martha Drabsche.

The seven Chambers children circa 1936.
Back L-R Bill, Colin, Jack, Alf.
Front L-R Olive, Harry, Daisy.

2.

The Youth of Lucy McLaren

Lucy's early childhood was anything but happy. Born on the last day of September in 1899, her birthdays progressed along with the new century. Her parents were John and Claire McLaren in the New South Wales town of Glen Innes and she was the sixth child in a family of seven. There were three older sons Alex, John and William and two girls, Mary and Margaret, who were two and four years older than Lucy, then Clara, the baby of the family.

Hard times caused strained circumstances between the parents and they split up. While her husband and the three older boys were away on contract work the mother deserted the four little girls, leaving them in the house on their own. Lucy was only six years old and the experience was so devastating that she never wished to talk about it. She preferred to live for the future and forget the past.

Eventually a kindly neighbour, Martha Drabsche, found the girls alone in the house with no food. They were so desperately hungry that they ate frogs grilled on top of the wood stove to stay alive. Martha Drabsche fostered Mary, the oldest girl and Clara the youngest but they retained the McLaren name. Martha, her husband and family were planning to go off to Queensland to select land for dairy farming and Mary and Clara soon found themselves there.

Martha's eldest daughter Sara Hiscox and her gentle giant of a husband, Jack, fostered Lucy as they had no children of their own. The family remained around the Glen Innes area for a few years where Jack worked on stations with his horse-drawn tip-dray. The couple soon became very fond of their adopted daughter. The other sister, Margaret, was adopted by the local Winstanly family and also remained in New South Wales.

Jack Hiscox was an excellent axeman and general handyman and had his own horses and tip-dray and took work on 'Ben Loman' station in the high country near Gyra. He worked at many jobs, such as cord wood hauling for steam engines, road making and sinking small dams. At shearing or lambing time, he was always called upon to help with the sheep, much to the delight of his foster daughter, who simply adored animals. Jack bought her a quiet little pony mare, Jenny, and later a very light, two-wheeled dog cart which the pony could pull. Lucy became a remarkably smart little horse-woman, and earned pocket money by helping to muster sheep as well as trapping rabbits and the occasional fox. Killing foxes with a long handled shovel before removing them from a trap, took some courage for an eight year old girl.

Jack could only muster sheep in untimbered country because he was always too heavy for horse riding, tipping the scales at twenty-three stone. To muster he drove the tip-dray and used a good sheep dog. Both his legs were broken when he was hit by the cow fender of a train. The fractures didn't mend straight so he was lame. Leaning heavily on poorly constructed crutches had also damaged the nerves in his armpits and almost resulted in him losing the use of his arms. Lucy was the apple of his eye. She assisted him working sheep on her pony, so despite his disabilities he dreamed of having his own sheep run.

Jack's first wife had died and following that sad event he had made a trip to Mungallala to see his brother-in-law, George Burey. While he was there, Jack selected 3,600 acres of country well covered with brigalow and wilga scrub and teeming with wallabies. It required a lot of work before he could hope to run any sheep. For a start he would have to dingo-proof it with a netting fence. It was on his return from this trip that he had the accident that damaged his legs and not long after he married Sara.

Before the accident he had excelled at woodchopping and won many blue ribbons at local shows against world class axemen, throughout New South Wales. Jack never drank alcohol but he had a sweet tooth and indulged in soft drinks and boiled lollies when he came into town. Being a kindly man he would often spend the weekends cutting and hauling fire wood for elderly people, accepting no more than a cup of tea in return.

In 1909, Jack decided to move permanently to Queensland. The tip-dray was loaded with furniture and sundry goods and chattels and with three horses in hand and Lucy driving Jenny in her own little chariot, the family set off on the 800 mile journey. She often became so weary she momentarily dropped off to sleep only to wake and find Jenny following close in behind the rear of the tip-dray. Little did she realise that this was a preliminary run for a future marathon journey. From the high country their route lay inland through Inverell, Texas, Millmerran, Dalby to Chinchilla. Here they stopped with the Drabsche family out at Pelican. Sara was happy to be reunited with her own immediate family and Lucy was delighted to see her two sisters, Mary and Clara.

There wasn't much grain growing in the area and the prickly pear was rampant. Back in those days everything had to be done the hard way. The most reliable and efficient milking machine in the dairy was the old M, D & K system — Mum, Dad and the Kids! All the girls pitched in to do the milking. The main product was butterfat and the skim milk was fed to the orphan poddy calves and pigs. Milk was put through a large hand-turned separator to spin off the cream into six to ten gallon cans. These were locked down and transported to the nearest butter factory. The farmer was paid on butter yield and quality at the end of each month. Goods trains picked up the cans all the way along the line from little cream sheds. These trains were so slow, they were called 'I'll Walk Beside You' from the song of that name.

Mrs Drabsche had an interesting hobby. She was very skilled at making papier mâché cattle and horse models and showed Mary and Clara how it was done. They were modelled to scale, life-like and minutely detailed. The hair from newly born calves was carefully brushed into hot beeswax so that it all lay in the right direction and the hooves and horns were carved from boiled sheep's horn. Minor details such as the hair curl in the middle of the forehead and the top of the shoulder blade or withers, gave each beast a realistic appearance. They were so perfect that an art dealer offered several thousand pounds for the models but Martha wouldn't sell them.

Jack had a job as a gang foreman on the railway line at Mungallala where he had bought the small block of scrub land several years previously. Lucy's stop-over with her sisters was therefore necessarily shortlived. Jack Hiscox's horses, having the benefit of the rest at Pelican, were able to cover the remaining journey effortlessly, doing good long stages to Mungallala.

At first, Sara and Jack rented a house in Mungallala. Soon a general store became available for rent and Sara decided she could run it. Later on they bought a much larger building close by the railway station yards, as a general store. Lucy was able to handle the bulk of the grocery boxes with her own small horse and cart. Heavier items such as bags of potatoes, required splitting into two sacks for ease of handling. The heaviest items were the bags of salt cured beef. Beef carrying the nodule worm-kernel was rejected for export and consequently was sold cheaply on the domestic market through retail stores where there were no butcher shops. Many local people bought it because it was all they could afford and being well cured it came up on the rail trucks.

The nodule worm-kernel was thought to be spread by the wild dog population which polluted small water holes where cattle drank. Forty years ago nearly every aged beast had them when slaughtered. The nodule worm showed up mostly in the brisket fat and some old western stockmen were quite fond of the flavour and Aboriginal stockmen relished them.

Hiscox's general store flourished in the hands of Sara and Lucy. Jack's brother Tom and his wife met an untimely death and their child, Claude, was adopted by Sara and Jack and then a daughter Nina was born. Jack's land was overgrown with scrub and although he erected a six foot dingo fence around it and built a dam he could only run a small number of sheep. Lucy tended them on her pony.

Sara branched out into real estate on a small scale. She bought house blocks in the town and had an aged local carpenter construct modest dwellings for rental.

These houses, which had neither power nor reticulated water, consisted of two bedrooms, kitchen with wood stove, a laundry-bathroom, a pit type backyard toilet and a rainwater tank. Consequently they only brought a low rental of a few shillings per week. Lucy was called upon to be the rent collector. She absolutely loathed this duty but Sara would never do it herself. The girl was often the target of abuse from irate housewives desperately trying to survive in the depressed times. Similarly Lucy had to deal with bad debts in the store as Sara always made herself scarce at such times. The girl hated these confrontations but was diplomatic and successfully avoided any great loss through non-payment of debts.

Claude and Nina attended the state school but Lucy had to be content with correspondence lessons which she did following her day at the store. Jack and Sara both played the violin and Lucy also learned to play reasonably well. Jack's old favourite was a tin fiddle, soldered up by an expert tinsmith from part of a four gallon kerosene tin. He delighted in belting out Irish jigs on this instrument and sometimes he and Lucy provided the music for local dances.

A young school teacher began to pay Lucy quite a bit of attention but Sara was not in favour of the courtship and smartly put a stop to it. However, she didn't object when the rather deaf but attractive, older grazier, Sid Chambers, called around. Their friendship changed to romance and so at the age of forty-two Sid married Lucy, who was the tender age of twenty.

Sid and Lucy's mud brick house at 'Lillypool'.

Sid trying to hit the emu on the head with the stirrup
iron. Alby opens fire, causing the horse to shy.

3

Sid and Lucy in Double Harness

After a short honeymoon the groom brought his wife to live at 'Lilypool'. The comfortable, strong mud brick dwelling was situated on top of a small ridge overlooking a large dam, built by Sid and his horse team, in Box Flat Creek. The creek only ran after big rain and then made pleasant viewing from the house.

The main structure had two bedrooms opening onto a long dining room and was warm in winter yet cool in the summer. The cypress pine floor boards were kept spotless by Lucy and her scrubbing brush. The ceiling was hessian painted with whitewash and tied up to a roofing frame. Sid built a pine, slab-walled lean-to with a cement and flagstone floor on the southern side. This was of a rougher construction and disposed as the kitchen, bathroom and a worker's room. To exclude draughts mud was plastered over cracks between the slabs and then painted with a heavy coat of whitewash.

Shortly after Lucy and Sid were married they went to town in the sulky to collect a palomino gelding, a wedding gift from a friend called Charlie, and lead it home. Charlie had promised to have the youngster halter-broken so that it would lead properly. As he was on his way to a job in his own back paddock he rode along beside the cart for part of the way. The young horse went along well following its mate, but when Charlie said a hurried farewell and jogged after some livestock, the young horse sat back hard on its halter. Sid had his saddle in the sulky and decided to ride the obstinate youngster rather than stress the cart horse by having to drag it along. Twice he climbed onto it and twice he was very neatly thrown so he hitched it onto the cart again and climbed into the sulky. Taking the reins from Lucy he said, "I had better drive, dear. This old cart horse might bolt with you!"

The newly-weds established a dairy. Good cows were not easy to procure, so Sid used a few beef shorthorn cows he already had, plus a few Friesian and Ayrshire cows which he was able to purchase. After a struggle to break in a reasonable number, Sid realised that Lucy was much the better cow-hand. When Lucy was milking, he put the milk through the hand-turned separator and then fed the skim milk to the pigs. One morning while doing this, he let out an awful yell. He had emptied the wrong can into the pig's trough. Finances were so tight every penny had to be saved so Sid furiously beat off the pigs with a shovel while Lucy salvaged what she could to put back in the cream can. When the cream went to the butter factory they received a cheque for first grade cream! The seasons were dry and the cows not worth milking other than for the pigs and household use so the dairy was short-lived.

Sid went back to horse-breaking and dam-sinking and gradually accumulated a mob of heavy horses for sale in Victoria. One thousand acres of his land was already fenced with dog-netting which enabled him to run a few sheep but in order to run more he need to extend the protective fence.

Within three and a half years Lucy and Sid had three sons. For her confinements Lucy went to a boarding house in Mitchell, run by a Mrs Fuller who was a midwife. A doctor was only called in an emergency. After the birth of her first child, Clara came to stay for a couple of months because Sid was away.

A few good thunderstorms produced some good grass on 'Lilypool' so Sid agisted a mob of cattle from drought-stricken Dalby. The stock belonged to a man called Isepie, and while walking the stock routes looking for grass they had picked up the dreaded lung disease, pleuropneumonia. Isepie kept the fact a secret and Sid put the infected cattle in with his own with disastrous results. The disease was somewhat similar to a bad influenza epidemic in humans — very contagious. It was spread by cattle who were carriers and contaminated the grass and water by coughing. Vaccination was the most successful method of eliminating the disease.

To save as many as he could he decided to inoculate the remaining stock against the disease. Enlisting the help of two local stockmen they selected a freshly infected beast, shot it and taking good care to prevent contamination, took the disease-laden, straw-coloured liquid from the pleural cavity. The liquid was put into clean beer bottles with a little glycerine for the next few days. A piece of knitting wool, three inches long, was immersed in a bowl of vaccine, then using a cutting edge needle on a handle the piece of wool was inserted in the gristle at the end of the beast's tail. Care had to be taken to avoid piercing the bone or gangrene would set in requiring amputation of the tail. The piece of wool remained in place for the organisms to be absorbed into the animal's bloodstream, thereby producing immunity. As each animal was inoculated, it was bang-tailed to make sure none were missed.

Calves, too small for a cattle crush, were scruffed in a small yard. While doing this, one chap fell backwards onto a virus needle and copped it right square in the tail bone. He claimed he would be all right, but Sid insisted that the newly acquired motor ambulance be called to take him to hospital. The old doctor, himself a property owner, found it amusing that the injury was in exactly the right spot to inoculate the cattle.

With the job completed, Sid went to Brisbane and his two employees asked to borrow his wagonette and horses while he was away, to carry pigs to their small farms. When he returned, he learned that his wagonette, with bellowing calves on board, had been seen going through the township at four o'clock in the morning. Returning to 'Lilypool', he found the wagonette soiled with calf manure and when he checked the agistment cows he discovered many with full udders and no calves. Sid promptly sacked the two men, but because they had used his vehicle he didn't report the matter to the police for fear he might be implicated in the theft. Rain fell again shortly afterwards and the agisted cattle were returned to Dalby.

Sid, Frank, and a nephew Joe Denton, did another trip to Victoria with a mob of 300 draught horses. With the proceeds from this sale they intended making the boundary fence more substantial. Sid knew the sheep wouldn't be really safe until the fence had a couple of barbed top wires and an apron at the bottom to prevent dingoes climbing over or digging beneath the barrier.

While he was away for sixteen weeks or more Lucy, with the help of her sixteen year old foster brother Claude, cared for the breeding ewes that were kept in a smaller netted area of open country. Blowfly strike was her greatest worry and with Claude's help she had to crutch and dress some of the fly-struck ewes. Lambing was timed to occur after Sid's return but if dingoes came around she was to engage the professional dogger. All cattle had been sold off the place because they made access holes for dingoes when fighting with their neighbours through the fence. The only livestock on the place were the few milking cows, and the draught stallion and brood mares.

The draught horses only brought average prices down south as the wheat season had been poor and the supply of heavy horses was greater than the demand. Sugar cane farmers along the Queensland coast were now looking for a better type of heavy horse and this provided a more promising market. However, enough money was made to complete the fencing which enabled heavier stocking with sheep.

Sid bought another 2,000 sheep which fully stocked the place. Come shearing time, things really got busy. The only concession to mechanisation in the shed was a heavy, wooden, winch-operated wool press. Some bigger sheds used modern mechanical plants, with flat belt-driven overhead gear, powered by a steam engine. Economy dictated that six or more stands were required to warrant running a steam engine so 'Lilypool's' first two shearings were done on the slatted board floor by a couple of blade shearers. Being an old blade shearer himself, Sid didn't think much of mechanisation even though there were a few two-stand shearing plants about that ran off an oil-burning motor. The noise made by the old, hit and missing Fuller and Johnson motors, more aptly named 'Farting and Jerking,' was memorable, as was the click, click, click of the blade shears.

At times when he was up to date with the sheep mustering, Sid grabbed his trusty blades and took a stand himself and made the pace peeling off the wool. Shearing was a drawn-out process and Sid finished pressing most of the wool into bales during the night by the light of a hurricane lamp. Claude Hiscox took on the jobs of penning up, rouse-about, floor sweeper and tar boy. There was only limited floor space in the shed, so some bales were stored outside and covered with tarpaulins. When shearing was finished Sid harnessed up a ten horse team to a six or seven ton wagon and hauled the wool to Dulbidilla, the closest railway siding, where it was trucked to the Brisbane wool sales.

Lucy cooked for the shearers and it was a job she found unrewarding. The grumpy old shearers, without a thought for a young mother with five youngsters, expected meals to be served precisely on time. Once when Lucy was cooking for the shearers she ran short of eggs to make the cakes and one old shearer volunteered, "Did you ever try curry powder in bush brownie cake mix missus? My wife uses it a lot. It is a good prostitute for eggs!"

After two years Sid engaged a couple of his nephews to do the shearing with their two stand mechanised plant. To offset the extra expense he made good use of his three older boys, who did the floor sweeping and penning up. Sid, who was wool classing alongside would yell, "Billy, Jackie, Alfie, run boys run." The shearers were amused watching the lads falling over each other in response to their father's stern commands.

The boys were now old enough to be useful and when there had been bad blowfly strikes, the ewes, many of which had lambed, had to be brought in for crutching. The boys mustered them and carried many of the tired lambs in slit sack bags, on their ponies.

The four Chambers brothers had by this time produced rather sizeable families with quite a majority of male children. One old town gossip remarked that there would soon be enough of them to start their own jerry pot factory!

Besides the shearing Sid frequently employed his strapping nephews Joe, Frank and Alby to do crutching and other contract work. He worked them hard and bawled them out if they hadn't done a job properly but they enjoyed working for their deaf old uncle and at times made him the butt of a few rough practical jokes.

When helping construct the last of the six foot boundary fence netting, Sid set up a permanent camp in what he called 'Gondah Corner' and went off somewhere for a long weekend. He came back to find his nephews had shot two emus right near his camp and had left the carcasses to rot. The smell was too much for Sid and Victor, an Aborigine employed at that particular time, so he dug a shallow grave and covered them with sand to smother the stink. Shortly afterwards Victor left the job and moved on and Sid reported to the police that he was no longer in his employment. He thought Victor would have gone the few miles north to the railway line but no one saw him go that way. It seems that he'd had a run-in with the police along the railway line so decided to walk south and made his way out to the Wyandra area.

Several months later, police were still expecting Victor to make an appearance somewhere along the Western line. One day at a dingo drive there was some discussion as to Victor's whereabouts and by this time the emu shank bones were protruding from where Sid had buried them. Within earshot of the local police informer, one of the jovial nephews piped up, "Oh! Uncle Sid shot him. Haven't you seen his shank bones sticking out of the sand in the Gondah Corner!" A day or so later everyone was quite amused to see the police officer come out in a buckboard buggy with shovels and wool sacks to exhume the remains of the emus.

Once while Sid was riding along his newly erected netting fence, he spied what he thought was the last bird inside the netting. Riding Captain, his very best stockhorse, he set sail down the cleared fence line after the bird, aiming to hit it on the head with a stirrup iron. Alby saw what was happening and hid behind a large box tree with his gun loaded. Captain was in full flight and fast overtaking the bird, which was now only about ten yards ahead. When the bird raced flat out by him Alby opened fire and the bird did several somersaults and fell dead. The horse shied wildly and poor Sid, who had been gently nursing a large carbuncle on his buttock, come down so neatly upon it that he promptly fell off. Soon after Sid got his own back on another of the nephews.

Joe was gathering dead eucalyptus leaves to kindle a fire for his quart pot and chanced to catch his fingers in a dingo trap Sid had set. Joe was so angry he took to the trap with the back of his axe. Sid demanded to know why he had destroyed a perfectly good trap and Joe replied, "They are cruel things. I pity the poor dog. It hurt so much I just did my block and took to it with the axe."

"Boy, it couldn't have hurt that much for you to be able to swing the axe so violently." Then Sid launched into the old story about real pain. "Let me tell you the story of a local chap who said he had experienced real pain only twice. The first occurred when he felt the call of nature and selected a nice quiet spot, undid his belt and pants, squatted down and dropped his testicles into a dingo trap.

"When was the second time?" asked a somewhat stunned Joe.

"When he bucked out to the end of the chain, of course." Sid said, "Now that *would* justify wrecking a good trap."

So far Sid had kept the prickly pear under control fairly well using arsenic pentoxide poisoning. Because his men were allergic to the poison he found himself having to do this job mostly on his own. Once during a slack time he had taken three men along to the pear block with the intention of cleaning up a sizeable area. After about three days he noticed them urinating and flashing their genitals to one another behind a bush and demanded to know what the joke was. One said, "Doesn't this poison effect you at all? You have been at it longer than us and we are all very swollen about our privates." When they dropped their strides, Sid was amazed and felt very sorry for them. He told them to stop work immediately, go and have a hot bath, change their clothes and go off to town, while he completed the job. The poison's only obvious effect on him was to eat the quicks from under his finger nails which always remained very corny.

When the new cactoblastis grubs were released down Chinchilla way, with positive results, Sid brought a few buckets of affected pear leaves home to 'Lilypool' as an experiment. He had such good results from this exercise that he ordered a dozen boxes of cactoblastis caterpillar eggs to be railed to Dulbidilla, for release on his pear block. The consignment was a day late arriving but when they eventually turned up on an afternoon train, Sid, with Jack and Alf were there to meet it. The little insects were beginning to hatch from their eggs and started crawling over everything, including the two kids. Instead of going to 'Lilypool', he went straight to the pear block and spent until dark putting them out onto the pear plants. The eggs were enclosed in small cigarette sized paper cartons through which a pin was poked to secure them to a pear leaf. Next morning come daylight, Sid had the whole family on the job. The caterpillars thrived, eventually cleaning up the entire area. By next season they'd spread over 14,000 acres of country. In a few years all that remained was the dried out skeletons of prickly pear plants which covered the ground creating a wonderful mulching fertiliser. Young Alf learned to keep away from the cactoblastis caterpillar because it caused him a severe allergic reaction.

The dog netting had to be ridden quite regularly to repair holes caused by old buck kangaroos fighting each other through the fence. For the protection of the lambs, the ewes were kept in the more open paddocks near the homestead, where they were under closer observation. Dingoes weren't the only concern, eagle hawks too sometimes carried lambs off to their nests to feed young.

To reduce the marauding dingo population in the large areas of cattle country surrounding their netting boundaries, an old horse was often slaughtered to provide meat for strychnine baits, which were broadcast far and wide. Some of the cattlemen didn't mind at all, claiming it helped protect their new-born calves. At the same time, there were always a few fellows who maintained that dingoes didn't get a lot of calves.

Though in some ways a great horse lover, Sid shed no tears after putting down a favourite pensioner chain horse or gallant old stock horse for the baiting job. He maintained an aged horse could have no greater honour than be the means of saving hundreds of sheep from an agonising death. It took a long time for Lucy to forgive him when Jenny, the pony she had from her childhood, met her end in this way. The pony was thirty years old and it was a drought year so far better to end that way.

Usually when baiting, Sid and the three nephews worked together. He always used plenty of poison to ensure the dogs got a lethal dose, whereas the nephews were inclined to economise, using a bare minimum. Sid warned, "By using only enough strychnine to give the dingoes a horrible gut ache and not enough to kill them, you fellows make a lot of cunning dogs that will never take a bait again." The nephews spat constantly when baiting just in case they got some poison on their lips but their uncle claimed that the powdered formula was not all that potent.

He kidded them a couple of times with a little sleight of hand, and got the reputation that he could take it without any effect.

Sid got the blame when the nephews borrowed his horse and cart one moonlit night and laid baits for the town dogs which had been randomly killing sheep. One chap had his dog poisoned when he came down the stock route and he asked Sid if he had laid any baits in that area. Sid said he had and enquired exactly where the dog had died. The chap said it had died on the chain in town later that night. Relieved, Sid said, "That would be the work of that damned young Joe. I always told him he never put enough poison in them. My baits would have killed the dog long before he got home."

One old bloke who lived about half way to town was a great dog lover. He kept many hounds of all shapes and sizes which he never tied up and they had been seen killing sheep. The dogs also menaced riders and passing cart horses and annoyed the nephews when they passed by on flighty young horses. One day they decided enough was enough, and laid a plentiful supply of baits in the area with very good results. This really stirred up the old chap and he reported the matter to the police constable who came out to make sure Sid was not using cyanide, a banned poison. The constable examined several dingo scalps plus a few fresh fox skins and was satisfied everything was legal. Sid assured the officer that he hadn't laid the baits. Although quite innocent on this occasion, he received a very abusive letter from the old dog owner up the road. It was addressed to Sid Chambers Esquire, 'Strychnine Gully', Mungallala. One sentence of the long letter read, "If only I was a few years younger, I would not rest until I had rammed some of your poison baits down your neck."

A couple of years after Sid sold 'Lilypool' to his nephew Alby it was noticed that when the rainwater tank got low they often got sick, so they decided to clean it out. Once it was drained Alby got inside and discovered two large packets of arsenic sheep dip powder. Evidently it had been slipped in there by lifting the gauze inlet. Fortunately the contents weren't able to totally dissolve because they were kept intact by a strong cardboard packet and grease-proof paper. The results could have been lethal. The only conclusion that could be drawn was that someone must have been murderously inclined during the domestic dog-poisoning episode.

One morning after making baits, the men came into the house for morning smoko. Sid had taken his boots off at the door. When the kid's kitten licked his boots, threw a fit and dropped dead, Lucy was furious. The victim could have just as easily been one of the small children.

When Alf was about ten years old, Sid took the three eldest boys to a dingo drive. Most places had netting boundary fences but there were still a few dogs about. It was surprising how quickly they moved around, merrily slaughtering sheep. One week they were in one area and the next they were through a couple of fences twenty or more miles away. The drive was on Albert's property in a 5,000 acre paddock surrounded by dog-netting in good condition. Plenty of sheep were being killed each night by what was thought to be a single dog which appeared to live in a thick patch of scrub in the north-east corner. About twenty riders lined up about 200 yards apart hoping to drive the dog out into open country into the guns of the shooters along the road. Although the dog's prints had been seen heading down a water course towards the other end of the paddock, the animal still had not been sighted by lunchtime.

After a most enjoyable picnic lunch, especially for the boys because there was soft drink and iced cake, the plan of the drive was changed. The drivers were to work in the reverse direction through another thick patch of scrub where the dog was thought to be taking cover and the shooters were placed further along the road in open country. Sid wasn't altogether happy with the plan. He assumed that the dog was cunning and when disturbed it would return along the water course where there were no shooters. Albert didn't agree, so Sid said, "Look, I will go back there to a good, wide, open patch on my own with my old .303 just in case he does come through there. If I do see any dogs, I will be shooting away from everyone else."

The hunt got underway. They hadn't ridden much more than a mile when the fire works began. Several shotguns went off in rapid succession which brought howls from wounded dingoes. Then there was a rifle shot away to the east followed by more howls. The nephews thought their uncle something of a hero when he got his trophy with an open sighted rifle at a distance of 220 yards, while it was in full flight. The projectile had hit the dog to the back of the rib cage, knocking it over for the second shot.

All the sheep owners thought it an excellent day's work when another much sought outlaw, a big bitch, was shot. This wily hunter had left nearly 300 dead and dying sheep behind her. In all, three dingoes were collected for trophies and a big celebration followed. It may have been cruel to hunt these fine specimens down, but they often killed hundreds of defenseless sheep in one night, which was devastating to the farmers.

Lucy was expecting her fifth child when Sid had a very serious horse accident. He and Claude Hiscox were riding home when a storm blew up. Claude was on a chestnut pony and Sid was riding an ex-racehorse. They decided to hurry and beat the storm by taking a bush track through timbered country. The young chap was out in the lead when he looked back and laughed at Sid, who was trying to hold his young horse in check. Assuming that the lad was laughing at the slowness of his racehorse, he let the giggle-headed animal go and it went flat out into a tree smashing Sid's head in. He was not expected to live and remained unconscious in the Mitchell Hospital for a week. When he regained consciousness, doctors thought that he would never work again and that the headaches and dizziness he experienced would eventually send him around the bend.

George Burey's wife Bessie was quite a few years older than Lucy, but they became the greatest of friends. Bessie was like a favourite aunt and took good care of Lucy's children when she went off to Mitchell for her confinements. In late

December 1928, the four boys, Alfie, Jackie, Billy and Colin were left with her when Lucy was expecting her daughter, Olive. The Burey's had an Edison phonograph which played cylindrical records by rolling them over the needle. It was encased in a wooden box and placed on top was a large trumpet-like speaker which amplified the sound. It was a source of fascination for the boys. An announcement was made at the beginning of each song, "Edison Record, Edison Record" and the caged parrot repeated the message to all passers-by.

With the confinement over, Lucy returned to Mungallala on the mail train. Sid still hadn't fully recovered from his horse accident and was trying to cope at home with the help of a man. The family got a ride out to 'Lilypool' in Stafford Burey's Studebaker sedan which was a rare treat for the kids who were only used to horses and carts.

Of the five children, four were of school age. Before Sid's accident it had been planned that Lucy and the children would move to 'Maroona' so that they could attend school. Sid had bought 'Maroona' in her name in 1925, just in case something should happen which left her alone, as it very nearly did after the accident. The move was delayed while Sid recovered sufficiently to be left alone. Now Lucy was needed at 'Lilypool' and had to work extra hard, helping out in the paddock where possible as well as giving the boys correspondence lessons. Her efforts in this regard met with limited success because they were always much more interested in what was going on outside. It was fifteen months before Sid regained his strength and balance and was able to carry on the general running of the property and Lucy and the children could move to town.

Lucy's small farm was good quality land with a permanent spring in a creek located half a mile in front of the house. It watered the horses plus half a dozen milking cows even in dry times. Water for the homestead and garden water came from a dam above the house. There was a small fruit orchard and they grew their own vegetables, meat, milk and eggs so it it didn't cost an awful lot for the growing family to live through the depression years of the thirties.

The new two storey home was constructed in the pole and beam style from cyprus pine. It had a verandah all round and the walls were of ripple iron sheeting that was inexpensive and popular at the time. Upstairs, the sides of the south and west verandahs were partly enclosed to block the cold southerly winds, thus making an extra sleep-out area. To prevent the kids from falling off, the remainder of the top verandah was enclosed with heavy netting. The kitchen and dining room was downstairs in the south-west corner and had a stove plus a rather large fire place for cold winters. At first the kitchen floor was only ant bed with lino covering but it didn't last long because the termites ate up from beneath. It was eventually replaced with a concrete floor which when hosed out, made a very cool area for summer living.

School days were tiring enough with a one mile walk to and from school morning and afternoon. Mostly the children were bare-footed and had to dodge the great expanses of galvanised burr. After school there was always some gardening or sheep work to be done and one of the kids always had to lock up the milking cow's calves so that the mothers could be milked next morning to supply the household. On Friday afternoon they couldn't dawdle on the way home because the horse had to be harnessed to the buggy for the journey to 'Lilypool'. Two boys generally rode and did the gate opening. They moved along at a brisk trot or slow canter and covered the twenty-two miles by nightfall.

As Sid's workers had the weekends off, he usually had a full work programme for the boys. Lucy liked to get away on Sunday afternoon at about three o'clock in order to prepare for school next day, but this didn't always happen. 'Lilypool' was overstocked, which caused an immense sheep stomach-worm problem and made a lot of extra work at a time when Sid should have been taking it easy. The worm drenches of this period were not terribly effective. There were all sorts of brews tried — nicotine and arsenic, sulphur and copper sulphate, and copper sulphate and mustard.

During the week Sid spent a lot of time on his own, cooking for himself. One day young Alby came to give a hand and found Sid sick in bed. "You're not looking too good, Uncle. What's the trouble?'

"Well you see, boy, after handling so many of those wormy sheep I felt crook in the stomach. I got around to thinking I must have my share of them too, so I took a dose myself — only a small one, the recommended size for a small ewe. Just must have been a little too much. It nearly fixed me for good."

"Good Lord, Uncle! That stuff is toxic. Just as well you didn't feel up to taking an old ram's double dose!" said Alby.

By lunch time Sid was up and about, though it took a few days for the effects of the poison to wear off. He reckoned that the dose made him much better, but Alby told him that this was just because he was glad to be still alive.

The sheep drenching went on religiously every month in an attempt to get on top of the parasites. A youth from town called Mick came to help for a while but he seemed to have no energy. He confided in Sid that he had worms but didn't know what to do about it. Sid was not game enough to recommend his own cure, so suggested an alternative method. "Now Mick, I know you are very fond of rum. When you go to town this weekend, go first of all to the general store and buy a couple of packets of epsom salts. Before you get on the rum good and proper and get too drunk, take those two packets of salts. The worms will all be that drunk, you will be rid of them before they know it." Strangely enough, Mick did try it but he was only game enough to take one packet and it didn't increase his energy enough to keep pace with his boss, so his employment was terminated.

When the family came out from town at weekends, the boys did a lot of sheep mustering and the drenching was done on Monday after they had returned to school. At half-yearly intervals Lucy conducted her own drenching programme.

All the kids were lined up and dosed with various worm syrups, such as Worm Phisico, Senna Tea, sulphur and honey, and prunes and some other concoction. All were supposed to be good for worms and keeping the blood in order. It resulted in the kids requiring clothes pegs on their noses to live with themselves, but thanks to the old bush cures they all grew up healthy.

At 'Maroona' Jack and Alfie often wandered around looking for bird's nests. They liked to blow the pretty eggs and thread them like beads on a piece of string. Lucy insisted that they were never to take all the eggs, only one or two. One day they came upon a silky looking nest swinging down from the branch of a mulga tree, far too light to climb, so they pelted sticks at it. The itchy caterpillar nest broke and showered them with its dusty contents. Alfie reacted violently, with watering eyes, sneezing and vomiting. Soon, masses of big red lumps appeared over his body. The boys headed home and were intercepted by Lucy, who happened to be yarding the milking cows, a few hundred yards from the house. She dispatched Bill to complete the calf yarding and took Alfie inside and suspecting he may have measles, plunged him into a hot mustard bath, a favourite home-cure for children with a fever.

The hot mustard bath stung like mad for a while but it washed off the itchy dust and the irritation eased. Jack told his mother what had happened and she was puzzled why he hadn't been affected. At first Sid thought it was hives, an allergy he suffered periodically, but he hadn't seen anything like Alfie's rash.

For a number of reasons there was periodically a shortage of hen eggs. On one such occasion Lucy was given some fresh emu eggs to use for baking. One emu egg was equivalent to eleven hen eggs. At that time there was a toffy bloke agisting sheep on 'Maroona', and he called in for morning tea. The sheep owner politely offered Alfie a slice of cake and to Lucy's great embarrassment he piped up, "No, not that cake. I want that other emu egg cake!"

Billy was responsible for the first egg shortage. He was being rewarded with boiled lollies when he delivered fresh eggs to an old blade shearer, George Gibson, who loved egg nog. George had a bottle of rum in his swag and would simply knock the top off an egg and suck it down like a big old goanna, much to the amazement of the watching boy, who then got his boiled sweet. George then washed the egg down with a sip of rum and claimed it all mixed into a nogg. A couple of the shed hands knew what was going on and tried to trick the old chap by placing addled eggs in the nest Bill pilfered. They hoped the rotten eggs would explode all over George, but he was too smart and sniffed them and threw them away.

Sid operated on a short fuse for quite some time after his accident. At one stage, after some heavy rain, blowflies became very troublesome. Not wishing to drive his breeding ewes far, he put them through a makeshift shearing shed, crutching with his trusty old blade shears. While bent over one ram, another lined him up, butting him right in the seat of his pants. He was unceremoniously dumped onto his head, in full view of the laughing nephews. Picking himself up, he grabbed the offending ram and drawing his sharp sheath knife, cut its throat and threw it over the rails out of the yard. Then he remarked, "He won't do that again. You fellows might think it a laughing matter, but I'll have you know that ram cost me forty guineas not long ago."

Sid operated on a short fuse after his accident and when a ram butted
him in the backside he cut its throat.

Men proudly displaying their dingo trophies after the Dingo Drive
(Sid Chambers centre without hat).

Lucy's house at Maroona.

4.

The Runs of Wide Horizons

Whilst living on his own, Sid began to think and talk of going west to look over Western Queensland and the Northern Territory. An old drover friend had often told him of the vast open expanses of well grassed, black soil, downs country, without a tree for miles. By this time Sid was in his early sixties, the time of life when most men think about easing up a bit, but his interest was aroused and his thoughts continually revolved around the prospect of getting away. Though by this time the cactoblastis had put an end to the prickly pear menace, the best country was continually being overrun by eucalyptus seedlings which required constant grubbing.

To satisfy his curiosity, he decided he would go and see for himself. First he sold his two places on easy terms to his nephews which set them up as graziers. Charlie agreed to take over the 15,000 acre pear block called 'Roslin' and Sid helped him boundary fence it and build a couple of dams. When 3,500 breeding sheep were shifted onto it from 'Lilypool' he was set up with a fully operational property. Sid was finally free to go north on his exploring trip when 'Lilypool' was sold, on the same long terms, to Alby, his brother Charlie's son.

When travelling by car with Alby to Roma to sign over 'Lilypool', Sid cut up an apple using his pocket knife. The fruit tasted awfully bitter so he tossed it away and then thought to check the knife. The thumb nail hole was half-full of strychnine but he didn't say a word to Alby. By coincidence their first stop was at Roma Hospital and here Sid commented that he was glad to be alive and told his nephew about the strychnine on the knife.

"Why didn't you tell me? I could have gone faster, Uncle," said the concerned Alby. "Yes, I thought of that, but on the other hand I considered you were going quite fast enough. Much better for me to be baited than have us both wiped out in a car accident."

The nephews often referred to Sid's pet aversions as the three D's — dingoes, drought and depressions. He was reluctant to step up from horse teams to mechanisation and although a wonderful old pioneer, he was perhaps born fifty years too late. Although he had never owned, much less driven a mechanised vehicle, when he decided to look for new land to develop he looked around for a suitable thirty hundredweight truck. In May 1935, he went to Brisbane and went along to the banks and reputable stockbroking companies, with whom he had dealt for years, and was told that they would not lend money to anyone wishing to develop country in the Northern Territory. Undaunted, he bought a truck and loaded it with petrol and diesel fuel for the Southern Cross No. 2 boring plant he had bought from Charlie Chambers.

In 1935, at the height of the depression, Sid left Lucy and the children at 'Maroona', and went on a tour of Western Queensland and the Northern Territory looking for likely country to settle.

Joe Daniels, a very hard working Aboriginal chap and a frequent employee of Sid's, went along on the exploratory trip, as his driver mechanic. Outback Queensland was in the grip of a drought when the pair set out for Cloncurry. From there on things improved under the influence of monsoonal rain. After crossing the border near Camooweal they headed towards 'Newcastle Waters' via the Barkly stock route, which was the only road across the Barkly Tableland in those days. The further they went, the better the grass and Sid's spirits rose.

Between 'Anthony's Lagoon' and 'Newcastle Waters' the abundance of beautiful Mitchell grass really impressed him and he remarked to Joe, "I must have a sizable share of this, so that my offspring are not constantly grubbing seedling tree suckers."

When they reached the north-south road they decided to have a look at the country down the Overland Telegraph line, to Alice Springs. The low mulga country round The Alice didn't suit him and he couldn't see just what the well conditioned cattle were living on.

The pair returned to Tennant Creek where they met Les McIntyre, a prospector down on his luck. He had pegged a claim about thirty miles out which showed good traces of gold but he had no means of carting water out to it, so he struck up a partnership with Sid, which included the use of his truck and gear, plus groceries. Sid stocked the show up with supplies, explosives, a water tank and petrol and after a few days a load of ore was taken to the crusher and returned a good sample. When a second load was delivered with the same result, it was suggested they all go to the mine warden's office and register their names as a working partnership. Les refused to do this and enlisted the services of the town pug to back him up. Sid and Joe didn't particularly want to get a hell of a hiding so they got out of town and put it down to experience.

The land around Darwin didn't impress Sid either, but while he was there he went along to the Lands Office to enquire if there was any land available for settlement. He was told quite abruptly that there were no leases available. By chance he met an old acquaintance and one-time neighbour, who was assisting Land

Commissioner Payne on proposals to open up and develop land in the Northern Territory. Sid was taken to meet Mr Payne and in the course of conversation he mentioned how impressed he was with the country on the Barkly Tableland. To his surprise he was told that grazing rights were available over some of this land at one shilling per square mile per year. Grazing rights-holders weren't automatically guaranteed a lease, even if they could prove they were genuinely intending to settle and develop the land and carry out structural improvements. Following this conversation, Sid looked over the available blocks along the north-south road and decided on the Cattle Creek block.

New leases were not being granted in the Territory at that time. It was considered to be all 'big man's country'. Land was for absentee landlords from overseas and the southern capital cities who put in caretaker managers and a skeleton staff in order to get the maximum benefit for the minimum capital investment. These big properties had very little in the way of structural improvements. A few worker's residences at the main homestead and a few wire bronco-branding yards and very little fencing. Almost the entire Northern Territory was one big paddock. Small men like Sid were not welcome, but he applied for the grazing rights, knowing that he would get no backing from the banks or stockbrokers.

Of all the country that Sid and Joe travelled, the grass on the Barkly Tableland was the most impressive. Returning via Camooweal and Boulia, Sid became increasingly disturbed that he had not heard from home. Although he regularly wrote unromantic letters to Lucy, reporting his day-to-day experiences, he had not heard from her despite always giving a forwarding address. When he arrived at Quilpie, almost home, he was very relieved to receive a whole pile of Lucy's love letters. She always expressed her love for him and her longing for his return, whereas the most endearing words in Sid's letters were, "To dear Lucy." He even signed off with, "Yours faithfully, J.S. Chambers." It never occurred to Sid that Lucy would have liked some expression of his affection.

Lucy managed quite well on her little farm while Sid was away and the family was almost self-sufficient. She earned money for wool, fat lambs and a yearling beast or two sold to the local butcher, so Sid was not called upon for financial support while he was away. With the help from the boys, the merino ewes were taken up the road and shorn in a neighbour's woolshed and the wool sold well. The boys also caught and held lambs while another neighbour did the marking. At about nine months old the lambs were trucked to Cannon Hills and brought a good price.

A cheap twelve gauge shotgun and Lucy's deadly aim provided ducks and galahs to vary the menu. When the galahs were in plague proportions she often brought down seven or eight in one shot for the kids to pluck. They thought the humble galah pie was good tucker.

Swaggies frequently visited, looking for a small handout of cooked meat or bread, which Lucy promptly gave them to get them on their way. An old sheep dog that put his bristles up to ward off cheeky tramps, though he wouldn't bite, was a comforting backstop when she was on her own. Much of the workload fell on the shoulders of the older boys. Jack was poorly so Alf cut and carted wood and did a bit of plough-holding, while Lucy drove the horses. He mowed two acres of lucerne hay with a scythe and when it was cured, put it in stooks prior to pitch-forking it into Lucy's small buggy. The buggy had a set of light shafts so that one horse could pull it. Hard work for a boy of fourteen.

All went well for a time until the mare looked around and saw Alf coming towards her carrying the pitch fork filled with hay above his head. This really spooked her. Colin was on the ground beside the buggy and had just dropped the reins that he was supposed to hold when she took off before Alf could drop the hay and grab her. Around the paddock she galloped even jumping a fair sized gutter, which miraculously didn't capsize the buggy. She returned past the boys going flat out and then ran into a deep boggy patch of ground and kicked out, got a leg over a shaft and broke it. The remaining length of shaft drove two feet into the ground bringing everything to a halt. That was the end of the shafts. They had to go back to a pole and two very quiet old mares to cart the rest of the hay.

Colin went through a stage when he was accident prone and Lucy wondered what would happen to him next. Sid had moulded an enormous grindstone using a sand and cement mixture. It was about five and half feet in diameter and had a square hole in the centre to which he fitted a square dray axle to act as a crank handle. It worked surprisingly well but required a strong boy to turn it to sharpen an axe. One day Col was cranking it when the handle hooked under his leather belt and spectacularly catapulted him into the air like a guided missile for about six or eight feet before he landed flat on his stomach.

Another time Lucy walked to town to help some ladies prepare food for a coming social event. While she was away the boys built themselves a good chariot by fitting a strong box with ten inch diameter wheels. Jack and Alf were harnessed up as the horses with reins fitted up to their necks, while Colin held the reins and took his position in the box as driver. The boys were galloping around the house yard in fine style when Colin decided he could stand up. This was fine until the 'horses' took a sharp turn around the tank stand. He shot off in an alarming fashion and rammed his head into a low sandalwood stump. The boy was briefly stunned and started bleeding profusely from a small head wound. Alf and Jack bound his head tightly in a couple of face towels then half-dragging Colin, took off to the bush nurse in town. He looked a ghastly sight with his head wrapped inside the blood-soaked turban, when they run into Lucy returning from town. Luckily Colin's injury appeared worse than it actually was.

Soon after Sid's return, he received word that the grazing rights over 1081 square miles of country, roughly forty miles by twenty-eight miles had been granted. Just a nice size for a horse paddock in Northern Territory terms. On receipt of this momentous news Sid decided to get together more plant and equipment for the land occupation. A bigger truck was number one on the list. Joe Daniels and Sid went off to Brisbane looking around at second-hand trucks and finally settled on a rugged, four cylinder International. It had the same motor as the McCormack farm tractors of that date and had no driver's cab, the driver and passengers sat on the tray. The previous owners had traded it in because it had solid rubber tyres which were useless for traction in sandy soil. The motor company replaced these with pneumatic tyres before Sid bought it. The truck was rated at three and a half ton but the inflated tyres enabled it to carry twice that and although it was very slow, with a top speed of twenty miles per hour, it had terrific traction.

In May of 1936, Sid, Bill, Joe Daniels and his wife and seven months old child set out with the required plant to start work on the new property. Joe drove the International loaded with the wooden Southern Cross No 2 boring plant and a quantity of bore casing which amounted to a load of well over seven tons. Sid, accompanied by fifteen year old Bill, drove the Bedford truck carrying materials for structural improvements, beds, a little rough furniture and general camping gear.

Seventy miles from their destination they called into 'Anthony's Lagoon', in order to introduce themselves to their new neighbour. When the station manager, Malcolm Newman, heard that they planned to run sheep, he asked, "Can you shear sheep? Well, you just can't go, until you knock the wool off these 600 or so jumbucks that we have here." To oblige him, Sid and Joe slipped in and took the wool off, which pleased the manager as he was at his wits' end trying to find a shearer in cattle country. Sid and Joe did his shearing for the next few years until the sheep were shifted to the Alice Springs area.

Sid was very impressed by the quality of the wool, which had very little fault other than a dust patch along the back line from being shepherded and yarded at night with a herd of milking goats. The 'Anthony's Lagoon' sheep flock never increased because despite considerable outlay for a dingo proof fence the dogs could never be kept out. The sheep were shepherded constantly by Aboriginal shepherds. Malcolm Newman, thinking the dingoes would be easily located on the open downs, employed an ex-army pilot, Joe Wilson, who flew a Tiger Moth, to destroy them. This failed because the dogs mostly came out at night. Joe was very daring, landing and taking off nearly anywhere and the Aborigines aptly named him 'Grasshopper Joe'.

When the party arrived at the 'Cattle Creek' block they selected the site for a homestead and bore, four miles north of No. 4 stockroute bore. It proved a difficult strata for drilling and after pulling out of a couple of holes, they persevered until they got a five inch cased hole. This was small for Northern Territory cattle water, but similar to that sunk on sheep stations in southern Queensland. The job took until after the wet season to complete and fortunately little or no other structural work of a permanent nature was done. During that summer they were plagued by diarrhoea and the water nearly burnt their innards out. Young Bill was the most badly affected. When the water was analysed in later years it was found not suitable for human consumption, although O.K. for livestock.

In March of 1937 the person holding the old 'Eva Downs' homestead block didn't reapply for the grazing rights thus enabling Sid to make an application for this better watered block.

Sid asked Lucy to come up and look at the property and she made her first visit to the Territory in May. Mrs. Bell, the wife of a travelling saddler and her four children came to 'Maroona' to care for the six Chambers children during her two week absence. Boarding a train to Charleville, Lucy then caught a Qantas plane to Daly Waters. It was her first flight and it took most of the day to complete. Sid and Bill, who were returning from Larrimah with a load of supplies and wire, picked her up. It was a slow journey in the International truck and they camped a night at a stockroute bore on the way.

Lucy's visit was well timed because the strong south-easterly winds which blew fairly regularly on the downs country in the dry season, kept the flies and mosquitoes at bay. When they arrived at the Cattle Creek camp, preparations were made to move to 'Eva'. The load on the truck was rearranged and some of the groceries were left stored in a tent to make room for more essential items. Before shifting, the casing was pulled from the crook bore and carted the twenty-six miles to the new site. This took up most of the ten days of Lucy's visit before she boarded the plane at Daly Waters.

At the deserted, old 'Eva Downs' homestead block, they found little more than a few termite eaten posts where a hut and yards had once been, and a mile-square horse paddock in desperate need of repair. At least there were reasonable-sized water holes along the creeks and although not permanent, they would last eight to nine months after being filled.

A few horses were kept in a very small paddock at 'Eva', so that they could ride up and down the creek to inspect the waterholes. The well was cleaned out and reslabbed, the horse paddock was put into rudimentary order, and Sid started building a two-roomed mud brick house. When that was done, a couple of wire tailing yards were erected.

When the Bathern place, 'Beetaloo Downs', did their horse-trapping muster at the end of the year, Sid bought a hundred or so horses and was loaned a couple of stockmen to bring them home. Without fencing, it was no small task for Joe Daniels and Bill to settle them down. They had been bred only ninety miles away as the crow flies and 'Beetaloo' horses were noted as home-loving by the many drovers who bought them. When they escaped, they had been known to travel great distances to get home. To make matters worse, the wet season of 1938 didn't eventuate and the paddock planned for their use was without water most of the time.

During late November there were a few light storms and Sid decided to return to Queensland, to bring his family and the prized draught horses overland to 'Eva'.

For some reason, known only to himself, he decided to go by sea. He caught the mail truck from 'Anthony's Lagoon' to the closest port, Borroloola, where small coastal trading vessels called. There he boarded the John Bourke and Co. steamer the 'Lisa' for Manangoora, at the mouth of the Wearyan River. Here it took on a load of good quality salt from Horace Foster's natural salt pan. Salt amounting to 400-500 tons, was swept up and bagged off the bottom of a big tidal lagoon which filled only at exceptionally high summer tides. Provided there was no late flooding, the water evaporated from the lagoon leaving the bottom covered with clean fine white salt. This was quite an experience for Sid.

The only vehicle Horace had was a tip-dray pulled by three horses onto which his Aboriginal staff loaded bags of salt to take to the jetty. There was no shortage of labour as there were about 200 male and female Aborigines camped thereabouts. They all worked in loin cloths, including Horace, who was a man with an exceptional physique. He lived cheaply in a paper bark hut, clothing cost him very little and he got an occasional killer from 'Seven Emus' station to augment his diet of fish and dugong. His life was lived close to nature and he had an Aboriginal wife and several children. The large tribe appeared to be under his control and of course he supplied them with liberal amounts of tobacco, flour, tea and sugar. Horace had a law degree and was to have been a barrister before he went bush-droving and scrub cattle-running. He took to the coastal life and tried his hand at Trepang smoking, trading with Malaysia in a partnership with W. E. (Bill) Harney. Sid thought him a truly remarkable man.

A couple of years later at the height of the wet season, Horace lost his life. Some Aboriginal boys got into a tribal fight and one grabbed a shot gun which had been given to them to shoot wild ducks. Thinking the gun unloaded, Horace said, "You fellow won't fight with this any more," he grabbed it by the muzzle and swung it down hard on a rock to smash it. The gun exploded, shooting him high in the thigh. With no radio to summon help the Aborigines made haste to Borroloola to get Mrs. Ruth Heathcote, the resident policeman's wife and an ex-Australian Inland Mission sister. Heroically she travelled the fifty miles on foot as fast as she could, crossing flooded, crocodile-infested creeks and rivers assisted by the faithful Aboriginal people. When Ruth arrived, she found that gangrene had set in and she was too late. She found a Bible in the hut and gave Horace a Christian burial.

After leaving Manangoora, the coastal trader's next port of call was Burketown, then Thursday Island and Townsville, where Sid took the mail train via Brisbane to Mungallala. He arrived a week before Christmas.

5.

The Gypsy Caravan

At sundown on the first day of the Chambers family's migration to the Northern Territory, the caravan of heavily laden, horsedrawn vehicles drew up alongside a small cow yard. This was handy to catch and hobble the inexperienced young horses for the night. The menagerie of chooks and turkeys had taken quite a while to catch, even within the confines of the hen house at 'Maroona', so they remained caged under the wagonette. The following day the seventeen miles to Morven was accomplished by lunch time, so the poultry were let out to graze. After being fed they were quite contented to stay close by picking about and that night they were taught to roost on the shafts and poles of the horse-drawn vehicles. In the morning after another pick around they didn't need much persuading to return to the cages under the wagonette, and soon settled to the new routine, even laying the occasional egg.

The morning the party left Morven, they had the first casualty of the journey. Olive and Daisy were very fond of their cat Tommy and brought him along. He didn't stray the first night, but on the second he deserted the family and went to investigate the bright lights of Morven, about a quarter of a mile away from the camp. A long stage was planned for that day so there was no time to do a house-to-house search as the girls wished, so they tearfully said goodbye to their pet. Tommy probably thought it was a good idea to leave because shortly before the trip Jack had coaxed the cat inside a riding legging with his head nearly out one end. While Alf held his hind legs Jack castrated him with a safety razor blade. Just when he tossed the first testicle away, three year old Harry chanced to come along. He raced into Lucy to tell her, "That naughty Jack is cutting meat out of poor Tommy!"

The horses were hobbled at night to keep them close to camp for easy catching the following morning. Young horses that were difficult to hobble were left with

Lucy setting out for Queensland in her buggy pulled by Jenny.

Daisy sleepwalking — "I fell out of the buggy."

a hobble attached to one foot, then Sid quietly slipped a long, strong but light hook attached to a rope, through the hobble. The boys and Sid held onto the end of the rope and when the youngster ran away it was tripped over. A couple of spills usually taught them to stand up quietly for hobbling.

Beyond Augathella there was plenty of good grass for the horses but shade for camping was often in short supply. At one of the stations along the way half a butchered sheep was bought and at the next camp there was a big cook-up in the cast-iron camp ovens, in order to replenish the tucker box. Provisions from 'Maroona' were starting to run out and the children were getting bouts of summer sickness or Barcoo biliousness from the incredible numbers of flies. Some of the station people were suspicious of the Chambers caravan, thinking them a mob of passing gypsies, so they sometimes found it hard to buy meat.

A couple of miles out along the road to Tambo the party was greeted by the town goats. The horses had never seen or smelt a goat before and they put on quite a performance. Who could blame them reacting to the strange smell of a rank old billy goat? When Sid presented his stock permit to the local police constable he immediately thought, "This fellow knows very little but is officious and will try to lay down the law to a man, so I'd better do things by the book."

There was no butcher in town, but they were given the name of a lady who had some young goats available. Towards sundown when the goats came home, Sid and Alf went along carrying a clean sugar bag. Soon the big mob of goats approached the town and gradually peeled off in their own little mobs to go to their respective households for milking. Sid slaughtered his young goat, put it in the sugar bag and gave the lady a couple of shillings for it. She then gave him a half gallon billy of milk which she said was "for the children". That was the first time the family had tasted goat's milk or meat and all agreed it was pretty good.

Sid's intuition about the constable paid off, because all was in order when he rode up to their camp looking just like a Waltzing Matilda trooper, putties, leggings and all. When he found that the stallions had side-lines on their legs, then a local government bylaw, he went on his way.

Some of the waterholes along the stockroutes didn't look very wholesome, especially those with dead bones about. To avoid stomach upsets, the water was boiled in a large kerosene tin and skimmed before cooling. In spite of all Lucy's care the kids occasionally got sick. Lucy too was unwell on occasions and it was most embarrassing, especially when they were travelling on open road on a treeless plain. She had to stop the horse and hand the reins to Colin, while she disappeared behind the buggy with a small shovel. The two girls held up a blanket to screen her from the traffic. Once the girls got a good roasting when they had an argument just as a car was passing and one gave the blanket a sharp tug causing the other to drop her end!

After Blackall the flies got worse. Near Longreach, when camped during daylight, smoke fires were made for both the horses and the family. For a few days all cooking was done at night and they had to eat their lunch under muslin mosquito nets to avoid ingesting flies. All the children wore bush fly nets, but even so there was still the occasional bung eye. Lucy tried to prevent the swelling by applying Ricketts blue, normally used in the rinse water after washing the clothes. Many of the horses too wore fly veils and an Iodaform/castor oil mixture was applied around their eyes to discourage the flies. They spent a lot of daylight hours in the smoke standing head to tail alongside one another — 'brush my eyes and I'll brush yours'.

The further west they travelled, the greater the distances between towns. Lucy was required to cook more at night, making bread in the camp ovens, also bush brownie and the occasional boiled plum duff. Sometimes wood was scarce on the open plains and when forewarned they carried wood on the carts, otherwise dry cow pats called 'buffalo chips' were burnt.

Past Winton the summer heat and lack of rain had played havoc with the occasional Chinese market gardeners in small towns, making it difficult to buy fresh fruit or vegetables. Water and feed for the horses was becoming more scarce and Sid allowed a 'know-it-all' ringer to persuade him against taking the usual stock route, which went from Boulia up the Georgina River to Lake Nash on the Northern Territory border. The ringer said that the route along the Diamantina River was better. The party found themselves wandering over rough and steep country past the old copper mines of Selwyn and Trekelano to Stanbroke country. This route took them well out of their way and added another 150 miles to the journey. It would have been far better to have stuck to the natural stockroute where drovers were still bringing cattle down from the Territory. If mobs of cattle could be brought that way, surely a plant of horses wouldn't have starved.

They camped on a waterhole in the wide channelled water course of the Diamantina River, which they were to follow all the way to Kynuna. The day had been very hot and tiring and soon after they retired to their swags for the night, a terrific electrical storm came in from the south west. Sid and Lucy were concerned because they were in low lying country and had to get out before the steel-wheeled vehicles got bogged. The children were roused and the boys sent to get the horses together while the others packed up the camp. It was pitch black when they set off, but periodically there were brilliant flashes of lightning to light up the bush track.

The storm passed a few miles to the south as they drove through the night. The younger children were crowded on top of one another in the buggy but were able to get a little sleep. Now and then Alf and Jack momentarily dozed while riding along and it was a relief to see the daylight. As soon as they were on higher country the party pulled up for breakfast, leaving the horses harnessed. At the next waterhole Sid declared the surrounding country too low to make camp, so the journey continued. Alf was sent ahead to scout for water and came across a small mob of wild pigs in a clump of lignum bush. It was two o'clock before the completion of the long stage at a small waterhole in higher country. Towards sundown when the horses were hobbled out on grass and the meal was eaten, Sid decided he would take the two older boys to kill a wild pig.

He had his trusty, old single shot thirty-eight Winchester rifle, but the pigs evaded the hunters by running into the low bush. Alf decided to run one down on his pony and gave chase. Sid screamed after him, "You silly young bugger. They will eat you." Alf had one in a couple of seconds flat and jumped off and tipped it over on its back ready to be stuck with the knife. Sid, who had read stories about wild pigs, kept ranting that a wild boar could have ripped him to pieces. Nonchalantly, Alf pointed out that this one was little more than a suckling and was easily kicked over. The kill was gutted and put in a sack which Sid carried across the withers of his quiet horse. He had a great deal of trouble persuading the mare to tolerate the bag.

Though the meat was lean and young and had been hung overnight, the children didn't find it very appetising. Sid, who maintained that he had lost most of his sense of smell due to his accident, declared the meat very good and praised the wild flavour!

That night, just as Lucy was dozing off to sleep, she heard a child cry down the road a bit. Sure enough, when she switched on her torch, one of the girls was missing. She ran down the road about forty yards, and caught up with Daisy, who was crying, "I fell out of the buggy." Strange that she should start sleep-walking for the first time in that area with wild pigs all around. Maybe Sid's horror stories about wild pigs had played on her mind as she went off to sleep. Colin often got up and talked and strolled around in his sleep. One night on the trip, before Sid and Lucy had retired, he sprang up and started running. When Sid finally caught up with him after a brisk sprint, Colin said, "I was only blocking the horses."

Being deaf, Sid slept very soundly and it took a lot to wake him, so it was just as well that Lucy was a light sleeper. Usually the slightest movement of one of the children would wake her. Despite Sid's many idiosyncrasies, he was a good father in most ways and worked hard to provide for his family. In the household his word was law but he never had to lift a finger to discipline the children. His stern appearance and a few words were always enough.

While travelling up the Diamantina River toward Kynuna, Lucy developed mumps. One side of her neck and cheek were so swollen that she found it difficult to eat or drink. It seemed that she picked up the wog from a shop assistant in Winton, who had a suspiciously swollen neck. Lucy had had mumps as a child, but according to a medical book it was possible to get it again. As a precaution she isolated her crockery and cutlery and washed them up last to limit the risk to the children. It was very distressing for her but somehow she kept going, taking aspirin for the headaches and using a sack of salt, warmed in the camp oven, to relieve the swelling.

As the know-it-all ringer in Winton had said, the horse feed all the way up to McKinlay was good. Sid was always happy as long as his pet heavy horses were full and contented. Sometimes Lucy was of the opinion that he thought more of them than of her and the children. When the little black bush flies were at their worst, he drove his team along with a muslin fly net over his hat brim and his pipe stuck in his mouth through a convenient small hole. He smoked black Havlock plug tobacco, cut from a three inch square compressed plug. He got the occasional bung eye, particularly after shoeing the horses when he couldn't wear the fly net. From McKinlay they ventured south along the Hamilton River down into 'Toolebuc' station country where they left the good grass country behind.

Several of the smaller children had biliousness and diarrhoea from time to time as well as extremely sore eyes. Sometimes they discharged puss alarmingly and had to be regularly treated with black agarol eye drops and cleaned with warm epsom salts water. When the children had bad cases of sandy blight, they became photophobic and tried to remain out of the bright sunlight. Sid had great faith in the argyrol eye drops. He'd been told that many soldiers in the French trenches during the war had used it to cure themselves of venereal disease. His brother Frank, a returned serviceman, had sworn by its efficacy.

General grocery stores were few and far between and the sheep properties refused to sell them meat and tried to hurry them on, so tinned food became their staple. The tinned butter had melted so often in the extreme heat that it was mostly oil and tasted very similar to the axle grease used to lubricate the wagon wheels. Full cream powdered milk was unavailable in tins so the children had to survive on tinned skim milk. Sid explained to the kids one day that the skim milk factory only had two cows, one was old blue stone and the other was chalk. Good for a person with a cholesterol problem, no doubt, but not for children. Lucy realised full well that her youngsters were not thriving on the iron rations and it added to her many worries.

The trail led them via the top end of 'Chatsworth' station, a property which bordered the rough Selwyn Ranges. Here the track was little more than a goat pad, up hill and down dale until they reached the deserted copper mining town of Selwyn. This once thriving area closed down when the demand for the metal fell. The only remaining residents were a couple that owned the post office-cum-store, which was very poorly stocked. Through the buck spinifex country there was little good horse feed or water and Sid came to the realisation that he had been misguided.

From Selwyn they travelled by the old Tricalano copper mine to a small patch of better country owned by an old teamster family by the name of Brown. They made the travel-weary family welcome to lunch and Lucy really appreciated being given a small quantity of milk and a few vegetables for the smaller children. Travelling on, they passed through 'Stanbroke' station onto the Wills River and followed it to Butru, an unmanned railway siding, where they bought a young goat to kill plus some milk and a few vegetables, before proceeding to Dajarra. This area was unsuitable for a camp because it had been eaten out by sheep and goats.

Travelling through such rough harsh country stressed the horses as well as Lucy and the children, but it didn't seem to worry Sid, who appeared to thrive on the gypsy lifestyle. Lucy sometimes reflected on her husband's ancestry and how much he resembled his mother, Eliza Jane, who was sometimes mistaken for a Romany Gypsy. When she watched him enjoying some horse trading in good old gypsy fashion at Dajarra, she almost believed he was a descendent of the travellers.

Lucy's greatest fear was losing one of the children on the long journey and she was constantly concerned by the frequent bouts of diarrhoea among the younger ones. A cold hand clutched at her heart at the thought that one of her children should end up in a lonely grave such as they passed quite often along the way.

Ernie Letts helped train the young horses for a couple of days in preparation for catching and hobbling at night and everything was fine until they arrived at Urandangi. Colin was kicked in the leg while trying to catch one of the young horses and when he dismounted back at camp he couldn't bear weight on it. The leg looked straight enough and several of the locals looked at it and decided it couldn't be broken. The closest medical service was 200 miles away at Mt. Isa. Providentially a local grazier who had a bit of country across the Georgina River, offered Sid some temporary work repairing dams and good feed for the horses, so the party was able to camp there for three weeks.

All the while Lucy kept Col's legs tightly strapped to a supporting splint and elevated on a pillow. Because the injury was so slow to mend, she suspected that there was something seriously wrong. After three weeks the leg was less painful when moved so they got under way again, following up the Georgina River. At 'Headingly' station they were welcomed by the manager, Hop Thomas and his very friendly cook, a Miss Anderson from 'Tobermorey' station. Sid left the horses standing in harness, while they had lunch and were loaded up with fresh cooked bread, a few fresh vegies and plenty of corned beef.

The following day, while they were heading for 'Lake Nash' along the Georgina, several mobs of travelling cattle were intercepted and Lucy and the children saw their first mirage. It looked for all the world like a distant expanse of water. It was so deceptive that it was easy to believe the story of Chinese gold miners perishing when returning from Halls Creek last century. The large party just walked straight towards it and perished somewhere north of Camooweal.

When they got to 'Lake Nash' station, Sid was once again talked into diverting from the planned route. Someone told him that the grass was better up the Georgina River to Camooweal, than up the Ranken River, which was 100 miles shorter. So up the border fence to Camooweal they went. There wasn't a lot of feed about, so occasionally a fence was cut to let the horses onto some decent grass.

At Camooweal there was a small hospital, so Lucy took Col to have his leg checked. It had been five weeks since the accident and the lad still couldn't walk. Without an x-ray it was impossible for the Matron to assess the injury and she wanted to send him to the hospital at Mt. Isa, where the leg could be broken and reset, if necessary. Lucy was in a quandary because Col was too young to pack off on his own, and she couldn't leave the other children.

Her dilemma was solved by the sergeant of police who had been an ambulance bearer during the war, and was called in by the Matron to give his opinion. He diagnosed a green stick fracture. As the injury was now five weeks old and the leg perfectly straight and both legs measured exactly the same length, in his opinion a visit to Mt. Isa wasn't warranted. This was welcome news to Lucy. Before leaving Camooweal, Sid wired Joe Daniels to meet them in the International at Happy Creek, twenty-five miles over the Territory border.

Before Christmas of the previous year when Sid had left for Queensland, he had hoped early storms would ease the workload for Bill and Joe who were looking after the newly acquired stockhorses from 'Beetaloo'. In early January, light storms did fall, making a little water in small holes along the Eva Creek so that the mob could be tailed out, watered, then put back in the horse paddock. After several sleepless nights because of toothache, Bill decided to leave Joe and an Aboriginal stockman called Victor with the horses while he went to the nearest dentist, in Tennant Creek.

With four riding horses and one pack horse he set out on the 190 mile journey. He planned to average daily stages of thirty miles. It was a long lonely ride to and from Tennant Creek. The only people Bill saw were the elderly Mr and Mrs Bohning at 'Helen Springs' and a chap filling the roles of cook, gardener, bookkeeper/caretaker, supervising Aboriginal women at their work on 'Banka Banka'. Bill reached the old Overland Telegraph station, seven miles out of Tennant Creek on the sixth night. The next morning he left his spare horses hobbled there and rode into town where he had the offending tooth extracted and bought a late Christmas card for his mother, which he posted before he began the return journey.

After arriving home, Bill minded the horses alone while Joe Daniels, his wife and Victor, went off bore-sinking. Their first job was for a neighbour Dave Cahill, on 'Shandon Downs' thirty miles to the north, on the head of Broad Creek. He was waiting for the bore so he could take his agisted cattle off 'Eva.'

Dave Cahill dragged a rough, home-made fire plough into the proposed site, so the trucks were able to follow up Broad Creek. They struck water at 310 feet before jamming the drilling tools. When they were trying to dislodge them, the drilling cable came out of its swivelling top section, leaving the whole set of tools jammed in the bottom of the hole. Joe wasn't an experienced driller and was unable to recover them with the fishing tools.

At this juncture an important bore in the middle of 'Anthony's Lagoon's' bullock paddock had fallen in, urgently requiring that a new hole be sunk before the surface water dried up. A telegram was promptly sent to the Toowoomba Foundry, who manufactured the boring plant, for a complete set of drilling sinker tools, box swivel and sinker bar. In the meantime, the boring plant was shifted from Dave Cahill's to the 'Anthony's Lagoon' site, so that drilling could be commenced as soon as new tools arrived. This bore was almost completed when Joe received the telegram from Sid to pick up the family near the Queensland border.

When Joe met the family at Happy Creek, the old wagonette and trailing dray were loaded onto the truck. Catching all the poultry and getting them into their crate under the wagonette, which was now up on top of the truck, was a complicated exercise. The truck was backed into a small embankment with sticks running up to the now elevated cage. When the poultry was finally loaded, Lucy and the children climbed on board the truck and waved goodbye to Sid, Jack and Alf, who were to follow along with the horses a few days behind. Sid drove Lucy's buggy carrying swags and cooking gear and Jack and Alf brought up the loose horses. Their progress was much slower than the truck and that night they camped near 'Avon Downs' station.

The truck drove past the old 'Eva' homestead site, where Sid had built a small house, to Surveyor's Hole. The well at the old homestead site, although usable, only provided a small supply of brackish water and as the season had been extremely dry, the waterhole provided the only available surface water. Surveyor's Hole was in the station's main watercourse, Broad Creek. It was a narrow waterhole, three quarters of a mile long and if early thunderstorms made it run, it was nearly permanent.

By nightfall that day, after four arduous months on the road, Lucy and the younger children arrived at their destination. It was Harry's fourth birthday. Lucy's eldest son, Bill, was waiting expectantly to greet them. He had prepared for their arrival as well as possible by erecting a bough shed and a couple of tent flies. Joe Daniels went straight back to 'Anthony's Lagoon' to complete the drilling contract.

Young Bill was caretaking 120 horses and Cahill's agisted cattle, and had half-completed building a stockyard. With the family's arrival imminent he had selected three shorthorn cows with calves at foot, which he hoped to tame for milkers. The cows were hobbled to steady them for a while and then put in a crush to be milked. One turned out O.K. One had too little milk and the other refused to be domesticated. There was no fencing to hold them so they were tailed by an Aborigine, Willie, on horseback with his wives Mary and Ida on foot. The first time they tried to yard them, the aggressive cow bailed up and took on all comers. Willie was full of instructions and urged his older wife Mary to go in with a nullah nullah, assuring her that the hobbled beast was harmless. It was just as well Bill had the foresight to take the sharp tips off the cow's horns because Mary was up-ended.

The children found plenty to do exploring their new home. On the top end of Surveyor's Hole there lay the remains of an abandoned 1928 Oldsmobile sedan. It had been stolen from Longreach when it was new, but now there was little of it remaining. Nevertheless, it was of great interest to Colin, who hobbled along to investigate it on an improvised crutch closely followed by Harry. It wasn't until 1947 that the thief was apprehended in Melbourne, on another charge of theft. He admitted operating under an alias and stealing the Oldsmobile nineteen years before. The police officer at 'Anthony's Lagoon' was sent out to 'Eva' to record the engine number for the Melbourne court.

Soon after the theft, Wattie Bathern, the part Aboriginal son of Harry Bathern from 'Beetaloo', said that he had found the car when mustering along Broad Creek. He found that it contained a good supply of shotguns, rifles, a couple of revolvers and plenty of ammunition, and a lot of tinned food and tobacco. The thieves were trying to get across the Barkly Tableland to Darwin or Alice Springs when they found Broad Creek flooded and were forced to abandon the vehicle. The creek would have bogged a mosquito in gum boots, but the thieves found a stony crossing and joined a passing pack horse droving plant as far as 'Newcastle Waters'.

Shortly after dark, several nights after the family arrived, the mournful cries of dingoes could be heard in the distance. Bill had just killed a beast and hung it in a bough shed by the camp and the smell of blood had brought them. Daisy and Olive began arguing about there being wild animals around. Daisy, the younger one, was convinced the howls were made by lions and tigers. Olive tried to tell her they were really dingoes. Harry sided with Daisy and it was all getting a bit heated when a loud chorus of dingoes howled from across the waterhole. In fright Harry shot straight under the flap of the nearest tent and came face to face with the stark naked form of Mabel Daniels, standing in a small round tub, bathing. He took off into the next tent and hid under his mother's bed.

Sid and the two boys took a few days to arrive at the camp. They found good grazing for the horses, but had to cart water a few miles when between stockroute watering points. Trouble was encountered at the Ranken River bore, where the trough was alongside the dip yards. After the horses were watered and moved on a few miles, they started to scour violently and passed an enormous amount of worms, so they decided to hobble the horses and camp. In the morning two horses were dead and others were sick. They hadn't eaten much grass through the night and at the bore they drank very thirstily. Sid was in a quandary as to what ailed the horses and wondered if the previous trough had been affected with the arsenic dip or if the grass close by the old dip yard was contaminated.

Apart from a few coolibah trees on the banks of the Ranken River the journey was across a forty mile wide stretch of treeless plain. At the next water-stop they saw their first steam-powered pump engine watering 3,000 head of cattle at the bore. Owing to the dry conditions the droving season was short and all travelling stock had passed through. The next two watering points were 'Brunette' station bores. The three bores between 'Brunette' and 'Anthony's Lagoon' were also well stocked and there were pumpers stationed at each.

There was a police station at 'Anthony's Lagoon' and across the other side of the lagoon, a general store in its dying stages. The owner, Charlie Biondi, was by family line a genuine Italian count, and had a growing family of ten children. At one time he had a thriving business but was sent broke when a considerable number of drover's cheques were dishonoured. Charlie was now in failing health and his store poorly stocked. While Sid tried to buy a few items from the old chap, his curious children and their pet goats looked on. Charlie was married to a part Aboriginal woman Queenie, whom he met when he was on 'Cresswell Downs' as head stockman. It was widely believed that Charlie was sent out from England by parcel post. His titled parents wished their friends, the absentee landlords of 'Alexandria Downs', to educate their son as a colonial cattle baron. The young man arrived in Burketown by ship and from there he travelled with the mail contractor through Camooweal to 'Alexandria'. Except for one short visit to his wealthy sister in Sydney, to head off her attempts to visit him, he had never left the area.

Queenie was very accomplished at whip-plaiting and other crafts but the generous handouts she gave to her tribal people at 'Cresswell Downs' helped to deplete her husband's finances. A close friend of the Biondis said she was quite a remarkable woman. Twice he was present when she put tea on the table and then walked off into the back garden carrying a couple of towels, and with the assistance of an Aboriginal midwife, returned a couple of hours later with a new-born baby in her arms.

When Sid and the boys set off from No. 1 stockroute bore, about thirty miles from 'Eva', the sky came over cloudy. Half-way to the next bore where there was some good feed on the cracked black soil, it began to drizzle so they made camp. The buggy was draped with a tarpaulin to run the water off and they spread their swags beneath it. During the night over an inch of rain fell. Much to their horror they discovered a great number of big red centipedes beneath their swags when they rolled them up in the morning. The area where they had camped was an outstation of 'Brunette Downs' called the 'Adder' block, which was notorious for death adders. The black soil had turned to mud and was heavy going for the horses pulling the buggy. This was the first rain the party had experienced in their four months of travel and they were grateful that Lucy and the children were not travelling in it. As they rode, the bitterly cold south-west wind cut through them, even though they were rugged up with rain coats. Their last day of travel was long and uncomfortable.

That night they camped at the 'Eva' homestead and next day the sun came out and dried the black soil road by about ten o'clock. Leaving all the gear in the shed they took a pack saddle of dirty clothes and a swag each and arrived at Surveyor's Hole Camp just on sundown. At last the long march was over and the family had come through it unscathed and were all together again. Now they all had to work to establish the property and make it into a going concern.

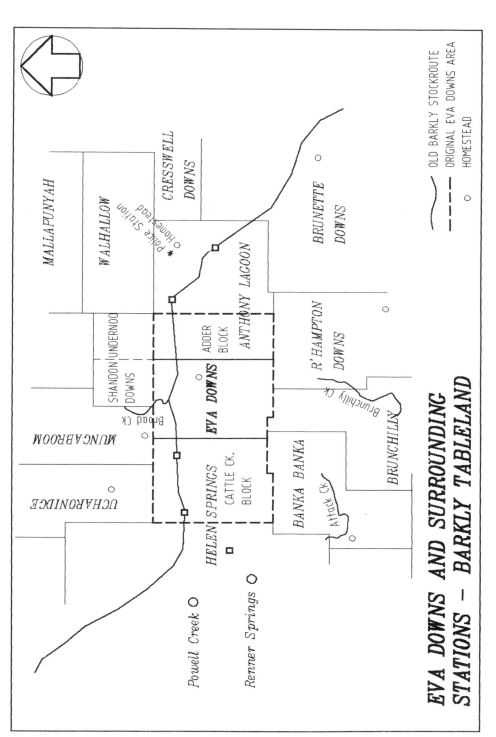

Map of 'Eva Downs' and surrounding stations.

Harry 'Bulwaddy' Bathern, Founder of 'Eva Downs' and 'Beetaloo' stations.
(Courtesy of Wally Bathern)

Part 2

The Battle For Eva

6.

In the Wake of the Pioneers

The first big job Sid got the boys to help with on their arrival was breaking brumby chain-horses. The breaking of these ill-bred, aged horses to scooping chains met with mixed success. Some went straight into the collar and were great pullers, while others were completely uncooperative. Sid's method was more suited to breaking in team bullocks than horses. The unbroken horse was roped and securely tied to a quiet horse, head to head and tail to tail. The tethered pair were then moved into place with a team of eight horses abreast which pulled from a wide spreader draw-bar. To achieve the greatest efficiency from the horses, the scoop or plough was attached as close as possible behind them.

All went well until they came to two obstinate horses, a large grey mare and a freckled, over-grown brumby stallion who although heavy boned had clean legs with none of the distinctive, heavy horse feathers. It had the conformation of a thoroughbred but was draught horse in size. Both horses were a similar weight and neither were keen pullers so rather than have them put off the keener horses, Sid decided to tie the two troublemakers head to head and tail to tail. A doubled piece of strong wire was tied on the tails in bullocky style.

When he tried to move the team off again, there was a revolt. In the ensuing turmoil the paired horses both shed their head harnesses and neck attachments leaving them attached only by their tails. The result was one of the greatest horse scratch-pulling matches ever witnessed. No one was game enough to go in and try to catch the wild brumby horse by the head for fear of being struck down and run over. Sid then produced a sharp sheath knife he always carried and slipped in close to the rear of quieter of the two, the big grey mare, to cut the tail hair to release them. In trying to keep away from the stallion's heels his aim was a bit high cutting off a couple of tail joints and drawing blood. Both animals dropped on their noses and then galloped off to the loose plant horses. They were a breed of brumby horse that were unwilling to pull, so Sid later castrated the stallion and he became a useful packhorse gelding.

That same year two coast-bred horses developed 'Walkabout' disease, which was always fatal. Evidently they had brought the wog in their system from the coast, only to succumb to it twelve months later. It was an agonising disease, the animals ground their teeth in agony and walked about aimlessly into and over fences, before dropping dead twenty to thirty hours later.

Sid agreed with Lucy that they should move from the temporary camp which was in a low-lying area near a big waterhole. It was easily flooded, a fact Lucy discovered after the first rain. Quite a few snakes were killed nearby, one a much feared death adder. This lent urgency to Lucy's desire to move to the old 'Eva' homestead. Joe Daniels had completed the bore sinking on 'Anthony's Lagoon' and brought the truck home to assist with the move. It was also used to cart good bore-water to fill a 900 gallon rainwater tank, which would last for a while if used only for drinking. The scanty supply of brackish well-water was drawn from the ninety foot well with a horse drawn whip and cable and was sufficient for bathing, the laundry and to water half a dozen horses. The eighteen gallon bucket had a trap-door flap in the bottom so that it could be emptied into a trough for the horses. When the well-water was found to be so brackish that soap wouldn't lather, Lucy had to do the weekly washing at Surveyor's Hole, twelve miles away and a terrible inconvenience.

The bush track Lucy used when going back and forth to Surveyor's waterhole, three miles up stream from the stockroute crossing on Broad Creek, was in fact the original Barkly stockroute. Although rarely used since the mid 1920's, the parallel cattle pads of the big travelling mobs remained. The gibbers had been kicked aside leaving a twelve inch track which in places was slightly overgrown. After the construction of the Government bores, twenty to twenty-five miles apart, the old route was no longer used.

From the 1890's, western and northern drovers overlanded their cattle to eastern markets. They had to rely on surface water, as this part of the Barkly was very dry. After leaving the plentiful supply of water at 'Newcastle Waters', they had a choice of several smaller waterholes which were not always reliable. These holes were Tandyidgee, Monmonah and Bundarra. After these, in good seasons, Surveyor's Hole was the biggest. From there they went through onto Cresswell Creek, watering at either 'Anthony's Lagoon' or the Adder waterhole, twenty miles downstream. In good seasons, they watered at a bluebush swamp on a more direct route to 'Brunette Downs' but if that was not available, they diverted south, to Corella Waterhole. The introduction of the sub-artesian bores removed the uncertainty of finding good and sufficient water for the drovers' mobs.

The boring contract was won by Syd Peacock, a Queenslander with a reputation for being a touchy character. He was ably assisted by his son Percy, who did most of the drilling, and daughter Lucy, who kept the books and did a large share of the cooking for the eight to ten man drilling team.

Peacock senior claimed to be a cousin of Harry Jones, of IXL jam fame, and so this commodity was in good supply in his camps, even though he was tight-fisted with everything else. He was fond of reminding everyone about his connection with IXL by occasionally remarking, "Harry hasn't made such a good job of that particular lot of jam."

Big, wooden-wheeled, table-top, horse-drawn wagons were used extensively but he had several trucks to get supplies and to run between camps. A wood-burning steam engine was used to power the drilling plant. It was a very efficient and economical machine, though on the Barkly where wood was scarce, it had to be hauled for miles in horse-drawn wagons. A plentiful water supply was usually found at a depth of 200-500 feet, then a pump-jack was installed temporarily, so the plant could go on to the next bore site. The pump-jack brought forth around 1,400 gallons per hour which was piped into a long temporary trough for the horses. Syd Peacock was most fortunate in securing Davey Cahill to construct the earth water tanks because not only was he a good sub-contractor and teamster, but he had his own wagon, team horses and scoops.

Stories about Syd Peacock and his eccentricities were many and varied. Percy was not above telling tales about his father. When coming out west, they came upon a packhorse bagman's camp at a river crossing, above 'Anthony's Lagoon'. The bagman was not about, but he had a bough windbreak erected and a fire going with a damper baking in a camp oven. Old Peacock got out of his truck lifted the lid of the hot, cast iron oven and tapped the baking damper and found it nicely cooked. He tossed it onto the seat of the truck, put the lid back on the camp oven and drove off. Syd, driving away with the stolen goods, nonchalantly passed the bagman returning to his camp from the station where he had gone for meat to have with his damper.

The Peacock family soon repaired the fencing on 'Eva's' one mile square horse paddock. They let some team horses go in there for a spell and checked on them now and then. The old chap went off to perform this duty one day and that night he greeted the men with, "Had a stroke of luck today. Got onto some very nice ducks. Lucy has prepared them into a large curry for all of you." Everyone enjoyed the curry and thought the flavour excellent, but next morning one man chanced to investigate a pile of feathers in the wood heap. Instead of duck bills, heads and webbed feet, there were Kite hawk heads and clawed talons. The hawks were nesting in numerous low coolibah trees along the creek in the horse paddock and the big chicks not being able to fly, were fair game for Lucy's curry.

The No. 3 bore was noticeably bad for gassing up the team horses, causing them to 'let off' alarmingly. The thunderous, bad-smelling blurts of wind caused the young Aboriginal horse tailer, Fulsche, to burst into great fits of laughter. Old Man Peacock remarked, "He is an awful heathen, that boy." At that time the water was pumped straight into a short trough and was still quite gassy. Later on, when it was stored in an earth tank before use, a lot of the gas escaped, making it good livestock water. It was not really fit for human consumption and couldn't be lived upon for any lengthy period. The next bore, No. 4, was even worse as it also had trace of arsenic. Further west No. 6 and No. 8 were all top quality water. Eighteen miles further on, the big Newcastle Waters hole was not known ever to become short of livestock water. To the west of this waterhole was No. 9 bore, on the edge of the black soil Barkly country. Davey Cahill's work ceased there because earth tanks would not hold water at all in the Murranji country and instead a couple of 30,000 gallon, galvanised-iron storage tanks were built on each bore.

The Peacock family completed half a dozen bores out through the Murranji scrub west of 'Newcastle Waters'. When they finished, they returned to 'Anthony's Lagoon' and put down a bore in the police paddock. This also provided water for a cattle dip used in an attempt to stop the spread of ticks. It proved to be the worst quality bore water and the external bore casing had rotted out by early 1940. Humans couldn't survive on this particular bore water, though horses and cattle were able to do so. The thirty or forty head of police horses were perfectly healthy and seemed to thrive on it. Perhaps the small quantity of arsenic it contained was medicinal. Race horse trainers were sometimes said to add a minute quantity of arsenic to horse feed.

All the earthern water-tanks were fenced to keep out livestock by a wooden post and five wire fence, comprised of three barbed and two plain galvanised wires. Wood was scarce and the posts were gradually whittled away by drovers, packhorse bagmen and passing motorists, who stopped for a meal or a night camp. After a number of years, the wooden posts were so depleted that Works and Housing replaced them with old bore pipe. In 1938, when Alf first travelled this route the old posts had been replaced and the only evidence of the former fence were four lines of wooden stumps, barely protruding from the ground.

About seventeen miles to the west of the 'Eva Downs' homestead on the stockroute in the middle of a vast Mitchell grass plain, there was a lonely grave. The road which lead directly to and from it made a sharp detour around the sacred plot of land. 'Boomerang' Jack Brady was buried exactly there after he died of malaria on Christmas Eve, 1923. The neat marble headstone was erected by his sister, Mrs. Whitaker.

With no trees for miles, drovers passing through sometimes carried a few sticks of wood on their packhorses to make a camp fire. The steel post and rail fence surrounding the grave provided an ideal place to hitch the night horses. The drovers knew that old 'Boomerang' wouldn't mind as he had been a fabled drover and horseman in his day.

Jack Brady was a brilliant horseman and came to the Territory as a drover in the early 1880's with what was Australia's biggest movement of cattle. Nat Buchanan was in charge of bringing 20,000 head of Queensland cattle, divided into ten separate mobs, for delivery to Fisher and Lyons leases in the Top End. Jack was a tall man with very bowed legs which he could wrap around an outlaw horse so effectively that he was seldom thrown.

Several years prior to his death, Jack, who was travelling on his own, once again broke both his legs. He was fortunate to be found by Wally Langdon — later Constable Langdon — who was awarded a medal of merit for his work in capturing the notorious Nemarluk. At the time of the accident Wally was a stockman on 'Newcastle Waters' and out track-riding cattle. He was alerted when he came upon a saddled horse with one stirrup flipped over the saddle and other horses complete with pack saddles. After searching around he discovered Jack lying in the grass with two broken legs. A note was sent to the station for a buckboard to bring him in.

A team of stockroute maintenance-men were at the station with nothing to do because of the wet, so they nursed 'Boomerang'. One of these men, Tim Dooley, said that he was a pretty fiery patient and thought this could be due in part to the rough nursing care he received. Nevertheless, the patient survived and went to Queensland to convalesce with his sister. While there he amused himself by going to the races and decided to bring down a promising horse he had out on 'Inverway', to clean up at the southern meetings. That is just what he was doing when he had an attack of malaria at 'Newcastle Waters'.

His friends tried to persuade him not to continue until he had fully recovered but he was anxious to get through before the wet set in. 'Boomerang' and an Aboriginal stockman were travelling along the stockroute on 'Eva Downs' with a plant of horses when he fell so ill, he got off his horse and died. The loyal stockman covered the body with a tarpaulin and took 'Boomerang's' wallet and delivered it to the police at 'Anthony's Lagoon' next day. The monsoon arrived that night so it was six days before the policeman and his troopers could get back to the body. Had it been rolled in the tarpaulin rather than merely covered it could have been removed from the track for burial but as it was all that could be done was dig the grave next to the body and roll it in. Brady's ghost was often referred to by stockmen who camped by his lonely grave.

For passing close in dim half-light
And riding a coal black steed,
A phantom rider, all glowing white,
Was racing to swing the lead.
It was Brady's spirits, I knew full well,
As the ghostly pair sped on,
And the black horse flew like a bat from Hell,
The way the lead had gone.

Bruce Forbes Simpson.

Once when a storm was building in the south-east, Alf was driving horses west along the stockroute at a good jogging rate. The first few scuds of rain came over leaving pools of water on the road and just as he passed Brady's grave, a large mob of whistle ducks rose up from it, screeching weirdly. The horses shied and bolted in every direction and Alf got a hell of a fright and for one brief moment believed in Brady's ghost.

On washing days at Surveyor's Hole, Lucy rose at four o'clock in the morning. The wagonette was loaded up with the trusty old wood-fired copper, buckets, tubs and an enormous pile of washing. One of the girls went along to help and one of the boys rode in the lead. When nearing the waterhole, the rider went ahead to light a fire for a cup of tea and collect wood for the copper. The wagonette was then used to cart water in forty-four gallon drums for the copper and to rinse the clothes. When the livestock made the water murky, it was cleared by immersing lighted firesticks in it. This was a method used by the Aborigines and helped a bit but made the water very hard.

Once when Jack and Colin were carting the wash water, they took some soap and decided to soak in the shallow water. After a while they realised that a large snake was doing the same thing. They flew out onto the dry bank and watched the snake and killed it as it emerged. The trophy was taken home and found to measure seven foot three inches. Being unfamiliar with the local snakes, they thought the huge, greenish brown reptile was a non-venomous carpet snake. Shivers went down their spines when later they discovered it was a deadly king brown.

In the dry atmosphere the washing dried quickly on a makeshift clothesline strung from tree to tree. While the clothes were drying and the frame for the copper cooled off, socks and woollen clothes were put through. They were put in a canvas bag and hung out at home.

The job was usually finished in time for a late lunch and between four and five o'clock they were homeward bound. Sometimes they didn't arrive until ten o'clock at night. Lucy kept this up for two and a half months before rain filled the waterhole in the creek near the homestead. It was certainly a test of her pioneering spirit.

By 1937 Sid had completed a two-roomed mudbrick dwelling with a breeze-way between the rooms which was used as storage space. The kitchen was a galvanized iron lean-to and got as hot as a furnace during the day so he added a bough shed to shade it. For this he thatched lignum, cut from around the lagoons, because they lasted a lot longer than eucalyptus. Water was sprinkled on the dirt floor to cool the place and to keep the dust down when frequent whirlwinds swept through. There was no flywire and at night after rain mosquitoes became troublesome. When they became too thick, Sid lit up his old tobacco pipe to smoke them out. Cheesecloth nets were used because the mosquitoes were so fine that ordinary nets were ineffective. They were hot to sleep under and during heatwaves were moistened to provide some evaporative cooling.

Sid reckoned a breeze came up a little hollow from low-lying swamp land and moved his single bed with mosquito net outside, about thirty yards from the house. If a light shower came over during the night he pulled a waterproof sheet over his bedding and slept beneath it. Sid's snoring was incredibly loud but it never woke him. Lucy hadn't slept with him for years for this reason. Once, in the small hours of the morning, the sleeping boys awoke to the sound of an old shorthorn bull roaring aggressively close by. In the morning they found that Sid's snores had so challenged the bull that it had pawed dirt all over him, while he slept blissfully on beneath the waterproof covering. The bull probably wondered what kind of creature was roaring back at him from under the covers. Sid had to admit that his snoring must have been bad to have so antagonised the bull.

Within the house there was very little furniture. One item much prized by Lucy was a very elaborately carved and polished treadle Singer sewing machine that she had been given years ago by Sara Hiscox. The model was rare and considered quite a masterpiece by the Singer Company and they attempted to buy it for a museum. The rest of the furniture was mainly makeshift. Kerosene crates were used for lockers in the bedrooms, along with rough homemade beds with a mattress on top. The smelly carbide gas lights were by far the best and brightest at night and as a backup there was always the reliable hurricane lantern.

The dining table was an eight by four foot sheet of black iron. The legs were wooden saplings driven firmly into the dirt floor, then sawn off evenly to make a level base for the top. Eight light chairs were improvised from empty carbide drums and the kitchen dresser was a masterpiece made from old kerosene boxes. Along with the cooking and household chores, Lucy supervised the childrens' schoolwork. Correspondence lessons were sent from Brisbane and the children did their work at the dining room table.

There was no regular mail delivery for despatching and receiving the schoolwork. The constable at 'Anthony's Lagoon' police station took delivery of the 'Eva' mail which came out on the fortnightly Camooweal to Borroloola mail service. Travelling bore-maintenance men, or reliable passing drovers occasionally delivered the Chambers' mail. In the wet season, a rider complete with packhorse, was sent on a three or four day trip over forty-seven miles to collect it. This didn't always meet with success, as the Borroloola mailman often hadn't arrived from Camooweal. Any number of flooded creeks and rivers could have often held him up.

Bill and Alf once visited the camp of a drover Don Booth, who was travelling west to pick up a mob. Booth was an exceedingly good cattleman who, with the assistance of his brother George, had run the mail service from Camooweal to Borroloola. In the wet season, they used a packhorse outfit and avoided paying agistment by using the conveniently situated but abandoned 'Walhallow' station paddock, to run their horses. This was between 'Anthony's Lagoon' and 'Mallapunyah Springs'.

The fortnightly mail run with packhorses was quite an adventure. Quite often when creeks were flooded, he had to make a boat out of his half a dozen pack saddles. He did this by laying a waterproof tarpaulin beside the flooded creek then placing the packs upside down in a line end-for-end, thus forming the ribs for an improvised boat. The outer edges of the waterproof sheeting were brought back inside the boat and the mail bags and swags were ferried across propelled by a couple of strong swimmers. The plant horses had to swim across.

When the Borroloola mail contract had last come up for tender, the Booth brothers lost it to a motor mechanic, Clarrie Hudson, who had come into the area working on the bigger stations. The Booth brothers returned to droving and left a good number of breeding mares and foals behind at 'Walhallow'. A huge grass fire, thought to have been started by the big rat plague, swept through the country. There was one theory that the fires started when rats gnawed at dropped match heads. Another popular theory was that urine in their grass-lined burrows ignited spontaneously. It was certainly mysterious how every station reported numerous grass fires throughout the dry season when the rats were in plague proportions. Fires often raged through that country. They were called bushfires but really they were grass fires because there was no bush to burn in many places. Sometimes they travelled for miles destroying the stock feed. The stations fought it at night along the roads and by backburning in order to save as much grass as they could.

At 'Walhallow' there were reports of motherless foals wandering about with all their mane and tail hair singed off. In the panic some were lost or deserted by their mothers and others were badly injured when they ran through wire. After this disaster, the Booth brothers took their remaining horses from 'Walhallow'.

Clarrie Hudson took over from the Booth brothers and did an excellent job. He ran a light truck and performed a few remarkable engineering feats to keep it on the road. Once, to enable him to return to Camooweal, he improvised a wooden wheel-bearing using only an axe, breast drill, a round file and a wood rasp. On another occasion a few years later he broke a front stub axle. To overcome this handicap he used a forked green tree stump wired under the off-side spring and axle as a skid. Clarrie was a genius at keeping his motor vehicle going and upholding the age-old tradition: "His Majesty's Mail must go through".

Clarrie fell in love with Charlie Biondi's second eldest daughter, Violet, and after their marriage he started his own motor repair shop at 'Anthony's Lagoon' as well as continuing with the mail run. He stuck at the job until after the war when Eddie Connellon, a pioneer of air services in the north, started a weekly aerial mail service to stations which had satisfactory airstrips.

As 1938 was drawing to a close a few storms made a little surface water so in an attempt to have a more permanent water supply the following year, Sid worked on an embankment below the house lagoon. The soil was so hard and dry he eventually resorted to a team of twelve horses abreast. The long heavy road plough took some handling, fairly tossing the boys about, sometimes a couple of feet in the air. They tried to hang on, while large clods of dirt as big as hay bales, threw the plough around. Sid urged the horses on and called out encouragement: "Stick to her boys!" They could well have been the models for cartoonist Eric Jolliffe.

Joe Daniels set the boring plant up over the old well hoping to find more water deeper down, which he did. Thinking there was now plenty of water, Sid started work on an earth storage tank but soon found that the water was far too saline for horses and that they would die if they drank it for too long. The boring plant was shifted six miles out to another bore site, where they struck good stock water.

7.

A Pioneer's Story

Around the time that Lucy was doing the washing at Surveyor's Hole, Sid detailed Bill and Alf to go to 'Beetaloo', owned by Harry Bathern. They were to buy a few more horses and collect those that had returned to the country of their birth during the wet season. It was a 260 mile round trip turned into 480 miles when they had to go on to 'O.T.' station.

After a week they rode out of low-lying coolibah and guttapercha country and were surprised to discover themselves alongside a large expanse of water in a big lagoon. Looking up, they saw nine or ten primitive buildings with high-pitched, grass-thatched roofs sited on a well-drained gravel ridge. Behind this was a dense clump of bulwaddy or hedgewood timber in which was a camp of Aboriginal people who mainly worked on the station. Naturally, there were a number of children and elderly people who were too old to work.

Among the main buildings was a larger dwelling built from split lancewood in a log cabin style. This had a flagstone floor and a galvanised iron roof and was where the old chap Harry Bathern, or 'Bulwaddy' as he was known, lived alone with the general stores and the station books. Although he couldn't read or write he always kept close control of the records. Harry was born in the little town of Beetaloo in South Australia, seventy-seven years before and had never been to school.

This truly amazing old man had lived all his adult life among the Aboriginal people and he was their supreme commander. Whatever he said was law. When he gave an order they immediately sprang to attention to carry it out, including his mixed-blood sons and daughter. Harry was small in stature, five feet five inches tall and slightly built, but he had the loudest voice imaginable.

The boys had started to pull the packs off, before the old chap hobbled down to meet them. "Put those packs back on and bring them back up to the huts. You can't camp down here. Your Dad wouldn't let me camp down on the creek, if I went to his place." So up they went and put all the gear in a building. "That is where Ernie

Sid's snores so antagonised the bull that it roared
aggressively and pawed up the dirt at his bedside.

Sid breaking-in his brumby chain horses. "He cut the tail hair to release them and both animals dropped on their noses then galloped off."

the bookkeeper and a couple of single chaps camp," he carried on. "They will look after you. There are plenty of spare bunks. Throw your swags on any one of them and make yourselves at home."

The beds were built in rough bush style from five inch bauhinia posts. Round lancewood sides, head and foot rails were trimmed and fitted and strips of rawhide were cross-woven to make the stretcher base. It certainly had no inner spring, but was softer than the usual chain-wire stretcher.

The three married, mixed-blood stockmen had separate cottages. There was a saddle and harness shed and a butcher's shop roughly gauzed-in. Each morning, it was the custom for the old bookkeeper to dole out the day's beef ration for the kitchen, various households and the working Aborigines. 'Bulwaddy' sometimes went along to dole out the rations himself to ensure they didn't get too much. He couldn't abide waste. "They would have us killing a beast every other day — just wasting beef allowing a lot to rot," he grumbled.

After living out of pack bags for over a week, the lads were looking forward to a good cooked meal. Instead the meal served in the station kitchen was steak and damper with no butter. Afterwards the old chap passed out some black treacle saying, "I guess you would like some jam on your bread, young fellows. It's a bit dry, so put some cream on it." Whereupon he passed a jug of goat's milk. The boys felt a bit cheated that he called treacle, jam and goat's milk, cream.

Old Ernie Wyndham, the bookkeeper, went off to sleep soon after the meal. 'Bulwaddy' was crippled with arthritis and almost blind and Ernie was his dog's body. "Dress me! Read to me!" he commanded Ernie. One of Ernie's many tasks was to read the newspaper out loud and once when the old chap had swallowed a fly, Ernie was instructed to examine what Harry coughed up with a small stick. "Did I get him Ernie?" Then he went into another paroxysm of coughing and spluttering to produce more evidence for nurse Ernie to investigate. He sure couldn't stomach the flies.

Harry, like most old bushmen, loved to yarn, so when they retired to the single men's quarters, he sat talking to them long into the night. The old chap told riveting stories of the early days. Apparently he had been approached a few times by interested journalists, but he just clammed up and they got no stories out of him.

He arrived in the country with one of the first mobs of cattle to come to 'Brunette Downs' in 1886. Drover-in-charge, Harry Redford, was a famous drover and cattle-duffer and was reputed to be the first person to open up the Birdsville track down through Coopers Creek. This feat was done with 1,000 head of stolen cattle which he lifted from 'Mount Cornish' near Longreach and took through safely to the north of South Australia.

It had long been said that Redford was 'Captain Starlight' in Rolfe Boldrewood's book *Robbery Under Arms* and some claimed Harry Bathern was Billy the Kid in the same story. This seemed unlikely. Harry was only sixteen when he arrived at

'Brunette' and continued to work there for a while before he went off with a chap named Bostock to start a new station further west, at 'Eva Downs'. Tom Campbell, a half-caste chap, who also arrived with the first mob of Brunette cattle, was thought to be the character Warrigal in the book. Who knows? A lot of stories got around in those days. Campbell started to establish a horse station on a waterhole called Undernoo, some fifty miles north east of 'Eva Downs'. His horse yards were eaten out by termites but the stone and mud brick walls and stone fire galley stood there for many years and may be there still. His horses were credited with starting a very large mob of brumbies on the southern part of 'McArthur River' station.

Harry Bathern, who was renowned for being as tough as the Bulwaddy tree, was one of the original settlers of the 'Eva Downs' country and had spent eleven or twelve years battling to develop it in the latter part of the previous century. Naturally he was very interested in the attempt by the Chambers to re-establish his old place. 'Bulwaddy' was not backward in reminding them how easy they were getting things. "Your Dad is giving you young fellows a wonderful opportunity, bringing you out onto that beautiful block of country. Especially in these days when you can sink bores to make plenty of permanent waters. The wonderful country is there, it only needs water. When I came out there, not much older than you fellows, there was no such thing as bores. We could only rely on surface water, which in most years did dry up. We would then have to shift into O.T. waterhole on the head of the Limmen River."

Lack of surface water was the reason, Harry explained, why that excellent grazing country wasn't settled by the big cattle barons and rich grazing monopolies from the southern states. When they discovered bad water in the well, they got the impression that there was no good underground water on 'Eva'. In his opinion the big boys treated the vast areas they held as an investment and never earnestly tried to develop it. He said, "You only have to look at the mismanagement going on out in the well-watered country of the Victoria River. Thousands of square miles of excellent cattle country is overrun with unwanted old scrub bulls. It is a big man's country all right. The managers are controlled by their pastoral inspectors from offices down south, who think they are big frogs in small puddles. They don't like to see the small man have a go for himself. Somehow the smaller man has to be enticed into this country before it will really start to go ahead. Mark my word, boys, if they could move you out, they would." Though uneducated, the old chap had a good head on his shoulders and a few years later his words proved true.

The old man asked many questions about the changes on 'Eva'. He wanted to know if the hut and yards he built were still there and was told they were gone, all eaten out by termites. Bill assured him that one thing hadn't changed. That was the sneaky cold wind which arrived in the mornings during the winter months. The early mornings were calm and still until you had just caught a flighty young colt to ride, and were putting on the saddle blanket. Then the wind would spring up from the south-east just like clockwork, and blow it off.

The lads were keen to solve the mystery of the skeleton of a horse, complete with collar, winkers and harness that Sid had found when cleaning out the bottom of the old well. They had come to the right person. Harry had often wondered what had happened to the young colt that a stockman was using to snig yard timber on 'Beetaloo'. It took fright and bolted to the place of its birth. When it couldn't find surface water it smelt the water in the well and fell to the bottom. Harry had trackers searching for the unfortunate animal for days and had often wondered what had happened to it.

Returning to his early days, he said, "It was really tough at first on 'Eva', breeding up all the horses and cattle. Then I had to breed the stockmen to look after the horses and cattle. Just as well they were a wonderful peaceful tribe of people that were there. I lived with them and depended on bush tucker whenever the horse teams failed to bring my supplies. I never had any trouble whatsoever with them. I was there seven years before they would grant me a wife, Queenie, who later became Angus, Hughie and Watty's mother."

Initially Harry had a partner on 'Eva', a chap named Bostock who had an Aboriginal wife and two children, Peter and Fanny. Bostock decided that having to shift to the coastal watershed for permanent water every two or three years, wasn't to his liking. He just walked off one day, leaving his two small children to be reared by Harry and the tribe. Both children grew into excellent stock riders and station workers on 'Beetaloo'. Peter was kicked in the face by a horse in his youth and was a little hard to understand in conversation, but he was a wonderful scrub-rider and horse-breaker. When riding a green colt in the lead after wild cattle through thick scrub, he had no peer. In the mustering camps the Aboriginal women played a big part, building tree-to-tree yards with lancewood rails and tailing cattle to make them quiet. Harry's daughter in law, Fanny Bostock, was an excellent hand at doing this, and had four or five other women under her command.

Story has it that Harry discovered the 'Beetaloo' country when in search of an Aboriginal man who had stolen his wife. Bulwaddy got a couple of his best tracking Aboriginal boys and a white mate, to track the couple through the bush. The fugitives were found at a big waterhole almost a hundred miles away, which he named 'Beetaloo'. The amazing thing was that 'Newcastle Waters', only thirty miles down the creek had been worked for as many years without the station Aborigines letting on about the 'Beetaloo' waterhole. Once he had seen the country, Harry was eager to select it so he continued his journey to Powells Creek telegraph station and telegraphed his application.

The livestock and his few goods and chattels were moved to the new station and he discovered several more, near-permanent waterholes to the east, so he made a 110 mile track through to the permanent water on 'O.T.' Station. As some of the water holes seldom went dry, he now had a good spread of country with much more reliable surface water than on 'Eva'.

The track Harry made was used at one time by horse-teams carting material inland from Borroloola on the McArthur River. When Sir Charles Todd found termites were eating the timber telegraph poles on the overland line, they were replaced by steel poles, which were shipped in to Borroloola. A depot was established at 'O.T.' Waterhole, consisting of a caretaker's hut and a horse paddock, where lame or sick team horses could be spelled. Later, when they were no longer required, 'Bulwaddy' took over these facilities. Once he was able to lease country around the better waterholes along the track, he surrendered the 'Eva' lease.

One yarn the old man told was of a teamster who frequented the track. Mark O'Connor harnessed up his team of sixteen draught horses on a fairly large plain one morning. He was in an evil humour and not on speaking terms with his Aboriginal offsider by the time he set off with his loaded wagon. Preferring to rely on his own sense of direction rather than speak to his offsider, he got lost. At sundown, after a long day, he discovered he was crossing fresh steel-wheeled wagon tracks. Finally he called up the Aborigine who was driving the loose horses and demanded, "Whose track that?"

"Me and you morning time, Boss," came the reply.

Apparently the horses had liked the previous camp enough to circle round and return for a further night's stay.

A lot of Harry's new country consisted of dense bulwaddy, lancewood and turpentine scrub in which cattle were inclined to go wild, making them hard to muster. As a result, there was plenty of horse-work tailing and spear-trapping cattle. The ZTZ-branded horses had bred up to nearly a thousand head and around the 'Beetaloo' water hole there was some four and a half miles of two rail fencing to trap horses. To discourage horse thieves, Harry kept his stock all well-numbered, branded and recorded.

The 'Beetaloo' horses were well bred, relating back to an excellent stallion that supposedly swam ashore off a ship wrecked in the Gulf of Carpentaria. This horse landed some sixty miles west of Borroloola, where it lived on its own on the coastal plain country. Aborigines from 'O.T.' told Harry about it, so he went down and saved it from the crocodiles. If new bloodlines were not introduced, the quality of stock horses or cattle on unfenced runs deteriorated quickly through inbreeding, so coming by this well-bred stallion was a real stroke of luck.

Owing to the quality of his horses, he secured a good price for them from the Indian remount market, and from drovers travelling through to Queensland. There was also demand for horses out in parts of the Kimberley country where walkabout-disease took a heavy toll. Out there, the average working life of a horse was thought to be about two years. Similar conditions applied in the buffalo country where hides were taken and sold for overseas export.

In dry years, 'Beetaloo' and north 'Newcastle Waters' stock camps worked together to trap horses around fenced waterholes. For some time wild horses were allowed to come in for water at strategic gateways. As they usually came in at night, a man was stationed up a tree where he waited until each mob had passed through the gateway. Then he flapped a white sheet to startle the mob, causing them to gallop along the waterhole into a waiting mob of horses being tailed as coachers. After sunrise the captives were taken to the adjacent stockyards. This went on for about four nights, by which time all the horses were collected and tailed out to quieten them. Young stock were branded and castrated and the suitable ones held for breaking. Those too old to break, such as some of the brumby stallions, were shot.

The station stock camp at the north Newcastle waterhole would often capture in the vicinity of 1,200 wild horses. One year some ill-informed sadist, who thought a horse had to have its ears pricked to gallop, decided 120 of these horses could be branded and then taken to water, if their ears were tied down. Holes were punched in their ears with a leather punch and a piece of wire put through the holes and under the horse's neck, so securing the ears down each side of the head. With fourteen men round them, the horses were let out of the yards. They began gathering pace down the hill and went straight into the waterhole, swam across and went bush. For years after, horses turned up with the 'Newcastle Waters' brand and two splits in the points of their ears where the wire had torn out.

After abandoning 'Eva Downs', Harry was surprised how both horses and cattle bearing his ZTZ brand kept drifting back there. As he said, "The quality of the country was hard to forget." It was natural for stock to drift in the direction of the prevailing south easterly wind. Some said it was because the flies were so bad. With their heads down grazing into the wind, flies drifted to their tail, where they were far less annoying. This was not unlike the Borroloola fly-veil principle, where the dead-beats were supposed to have torn the seat out of their pants to keep the flies away from their face.

On the day after their late night yarn it was decided the 'Eva' boys should go on to 'O.T.' station, Harry's other property, where some of their missing horses had turned up and were being held. Watty Bathern, Harry's youngest son, rode with them to check pastures, waterholes and cattle along the way. The 110 miles ride was easily accomplished in three days.

The soil became inferior, the closer they came to the coastal watershed and the magnetic anthills increased in number. They were all facing a roughly north-south direction, on a long narrow base and were up to twelve feet high. Bushmen had been known to use them as a compass to get their bearings. Dingoes were in droves and Watty shot half a dozen with a little twenty-two rifle he carried.

'O.T.' station was quite different to 'Beetaloo'. The galvanised iron roofing was a legacy of the days when it had been used as a team-horse spell-depot. It was situated on a very deep, spring-fed, crystal-clear waterhole in which there were freshwater crocodiles, up to seven feet long. This quite harmless variety of fish-eating croc didn't discourage the blokes from going for a good swim in the forty feet deep pool.

At the top end of the hole there was an area of flat sandstone on which the tracks of many animals and human beings were clearly imprinted. There were the three-toed imprints of plain turkey, emu, curlew and plover and here and there, distinguished by a fourth toe, was an eagle hawk and also a crow track. There were also well preserved wallaby, dingo, kangaroo and human footprints. They were thought to have been formed naturally when various species walked over a soft surface of silt which later hardened to a flat stone surface.

Fanny Bathern had gathered a lot of magnetic ant hills which she used to pave the floor and build the mudbrick walls of the kitchen. The meals were better than at 'Beetaloo' too and were prepared by Fanny's daughter, Queenie. Her husband, Bill Miller was manager of the station at that time. He was the mixed blood son of William Linklater, an early bookkeeper employed by Harry Bathern. Using the pen name Billy Miller, this well known old bushman wrote a lot of bush poetry and an autobiography called *Gather No Moss*.

His son was a very smart stockman and teamed with Fanny's daughter, he played a big part in running the property, after his father-in-law Angus Bathern, Harry's eldest son, was taken to the Leprosarium located on a quarantine island off Darwin. He was never to return and died within a couple of years. His wife Fanny, his younger brother Hughie, and several full-blood Aborigines later developed the disease and were removed from the station during the next few years. It was a ghastly, disfiguring disease for which there was no cure in those days.

Angus Bathern was a very smart, progressive man who, unlike the rest of his clan, wasn't under the old man's thumb. He had most of the dwellings at 'O.T.' built the same as neighbouring stations, with corrugated-iron walls and roofing. He wasn't as tight as his father and to ensure a change of diet from beef, goat, mutton and damper he kept a good supply of tinned fruit, tomatoes, butter and vegetables for use when it couldn't be produced on the property. When the poor fellow developed leprosy, old 'Bulwaddy' said, "There you are, I told you all that flash living gives people the leprosy. Angus wouldn't take any notice of me."

He resented Angus for building corrugated-iron buildings and was fond of commenting, "It's all right for an old fellow like me to have a tin roof to sleep under. I am old and had it. If the lightning struck that tin roof killing me, it wouldn't matter at all, but you young fellows have a lot of living to do. You never want to sleep under tin roofing. The lightning could strike it and kill you."

Harry at least made an attempt to educate Angus's two daughters. He gave Mrs. Bohning of 'Helen Springs' 600 heifers in exchange for educating and making young ladies out of his granddaughters. They were taught reading and writing for one year and spent the next on the road with the Bohning cattle. This education taught them to work hard and become good horsewomen, but was not what Harry had in mind for his granddaughters. He thought that for the price of 600 heifers the girls should have had more study and less work. When speaking of Mrs. Bohning he always said, "Mrs. Bohning was a wonderful pioneering woman who liked other people's calves more than her own."

After two days at 'O.T.' and with a few more horses swelling their mob the visitors returned to 'Beetaloo'. When they arrived, Watty found an engagement ring he had ordered from Angus and Coote in the mail and was very excited. His intended was Peter Bostock's daughter. Of course Harry had a few words of advice for his son, "Make sure, boy, that you get a good old Scottish parson to marry you. Not one of these English or Roman Catholic priests." His second name was Murray and he always claimed to be of Scottish ancestry.

Harry was never short of money. During the first World War, the story got about the bush that he loaned the Australian Government 10,000 pounds free of interest for the duration of the war — a lot of money in those days. Although uneducated, he was a sharp operator and seldom caught out in business deals. An Indian hawker, however, once put one over him. When he saw the hawker approaching Harry went to meet him with the intention of sending him on his way, before he could open up and begin selling to the cashed-up stock boys.

"Now look here, Mr Bathern, I didn't come here to sell anything. I am here to buy remounts for the Indian Army. Would you have any horses that I might have a look at to see what type you have?" said the hawker.

Harry's attitude changed immediately. "Oh yes I have a big yard full of horses at the moment. Come and have a look at them." The old Indian, who was a good enough judge of horse flesh, went through picking out some of the best of the mob.

"Just how many of that good, young, working-age type could you put together?" 'Bulwaddy' replied, "About 160."

"India is very short of horses. When you can put them together, get a message to me at Tennant Creek and I will come back to buy."

This put the old chap in a very good mood, "Before you go, open up the van. The boys would like to buy some of your wares."

The van was opened and the boys had a good Christmas spree spending all their money. The next day the hawker sent a message to Harry regretting that India had obtained sufficient horses for that year.

Another of the rare occasions that Harry got caught was just after the end of the first World War, when he was looking for a suitable bookkeeper, preferably a pensioner. A jovial wag of a packhorse bagman travelling through knew of another chap that was coming along several days behind him, and told Harry a sorry story about how this poor fellow had his testicles shot away in the war. Old Harry immediately pricked his ears. Poor fellow he thought, but he might be just the chap to do my books because he won't be interested in the young females about the place. When the bagman arrived, he was promptly given a job bookkeeping. Harry then went out mustering on the run for ten days. When he came back he noticed how familiar the girls were with the bookkeeper. It was a hot day, so Harry invited him down to the lagoon for a swim and quickly discovered that he had been deceived. When they got back to the office, the bookkeeper was given his cheque and told there was no further work for him. The poor fellow couldn't work out what he had done to deserve the sack!

Remains of the two-roomed mud brick dwelling Sid built on 'Eva'.

Old International truck with Jack and Dulcie carting water for well drilling.
This ancient relic is now in the 'Frank Ashton' museum, Mount Isa.

'Boomerang' Jack Brady's grave on the Barkly Stockroute on Eva Downs.

The Blitz truck loaded up with scoops.

8.

Up to the Knees in Mitchell Grass

When picking up the six monthly supply of groceries in Birdum, Sid met the stock and station agent, Fred Ullyatt, who was able to secure an option over a mob of cattle being cleaned off 'Mataranka' station. These mixed-sex cattle were to be mustered for delivery in June of the following year and were priced at one pound per head for cattle over twelve months, with younger calves thrown in.

When the supplies arrived at the station Lucy was delighted to find Sid had bought her a kerosene-operated Electrolux refrigerator. It was one of the first to come to the area and a vast improvement on the Coolgardie coolsafe. This modern appliance represented a step forward on the home front. The kids thought it was wonderful to have ice, although this was limited by the size of the fridge.

Finding the proceeds from the sale of his two Queensland properties diminishing alarmingly, Sid decided to get all the contract work possible to enable the family to carry on in the Northern Territory. Although he still had woolgrowing in his blood, he reluctantly came to the realisation that he was now in cattle, rather than sheep country.

The manager of 'Rockhampton Downs' to the south made an urgent and timely request for a bore. His neighbours, the White family of 'Brunette Downs', decided they required a substantial bullock-paddock for holding their yearly turn-off in readiness for an early start after the wet season. After each 'wet', four or five mobs, each of 1,200-1,300 two year old steers, were put together for contract drovers, who took them all the way to 'Tucker Tucker', their fattening depot at Muswellbrook, New South Wales.

A surveyor was employed so the fencing could be placed on the boundary survey. Even old hands didn't know where the true boundaries were, as the country had merely been marked on a map and never surveyed. In consequence, 'Rockhampton Downs' had put in a bore some years before, which was one and a half miles inside the 'Brunette Downs' boundary. The misplaced bore was now on the wrong side of the fence so another bore had to be sunk quickly on the 'Rockhampton' side. Joe got the job and took Bill and Alf along to help.

Towards Christmas the Daniels family indicated that they didn't wish to stay much longer. During the previous year Joe Daniels had found a sacred Bora ground and pilfered a storage log containing sacred sticks. There was talk among the elders of the old 'Eva Downs' Aboriginal tribe, now at 'Anthony's Lagoon' and 'Beetaloo', of returning to the area for a ceremonial corroboree. Joe Daniels, being part Aboriginal, feared a reprisal such as having the bone pointed at him, particularly as he had shown the relics to his wife, which according to Aboriginal law was strictly forbidden. Joe became increasingly edgy.

One morning when the lads were in the shed close to the kitchen door helping to grease-up harness, the eleven year old Colin made an innocent remark. Joe lashed out and slapped Colin's face and made his nose bleed. Lucy came quickly to her son's defence and sent for Sid. Joe apologised profusely and said that all he wanted to do was get back to Queensland as quickly as possible. While the Daniels packed their gear into ports and rolled their swags, Bill got the Bedford truck fueled up, then took them as far as 'Brunette Downs' to meet the mail truck on its way back to Mt. Isa. Bill returned that night just in front of heavy rain that made the black soil roads impassable for motor vehicles for the next three and a half months.

When the wet of 1939 started to take up, drovers began to come out west with their horse plants to collect their droving mobs. A lot of them still used horses and wagonettes for carrying supplies. 'Eva' put a plant together to go to 'Mataranka' for the cattle Sid had previously purchased. They met their mob approaching No. 6 bore, about seventy miles from home. They camped there the night and in the morning a very attractive brumby stallion was found among the horses. Jack was keen to take it home. The horse took off out of their mob and got mixed up in another drover's plant. His name was Charlie Schultz, and he was from 'Humbert River' station in the Victoria River district. Charlie tied one end of a rope to a tree trunk then climbed up and caught the horse very quietly by dropping the other end of the rope over its neck. He was broken in on the spot and became a good riding horse.

Charlie was a small man, a battler like themselves. He started out on 'Humbert', on the border of Victoria River Downs, as an eighteen year old in 1929, and this was his first sizeable mob he was droving for sale in Queensland. The previous year Charlie, who was a wonderful horseman, was a runner-up for the Queensland rough-riding championship title at Mt. St. John Rodeo, near Townsville. When he saw the 170 head of bigger bullocks in the 'Eva' mob, he tried to persuade Sid to let him take them on with his, for sale. With no fenced country to hold them,

Charlie knew that they would head back to the Roper River country as soon as the wet season came around again. He tried to persuade the old sheepman that he was better off getting rid of them before that happened and make some money. Charlie offered to put them with his mob, if Sid would provide one man to assist with the droving. It would have cost nothing and Sid would have made a good profit.

Sid ignored this advice just as he ignored the advice of Jack Guild from whom he had bought the second mob. When he took delivery of the 370 head on 'Mataranka', Guild advised him to sell a big quiet pet bullock. He said, "Look, old man, see that big bullock. He has been getting away from drovers for years. When we get to 'Mataranka' tomorrow, sell him to the butcher. He'll give you five pounds for him and you'll show a four pound profit. Otherwise, somewhere down the road a bit, you will lose him and he'll probably take a few mates with him, leaving you even more out of pocket." The inevitable happened near Birdum. The pet bullock went one night and took half a dozen big bullocks with him.

Sid paid dearly for these two mistakes made just when every pound was beginning to be looked at long and hard before being spent. After the wet season in 1940, less than half of these cattle were mustered. They had gone off with the bigger bullocks and spread over thousands of square miles of unfenced scrub country just as Charlie had warned. A severe financial loss.

Once the droving was completed, Alf and 'Wave Hill' Fred, an excellent Aboriginal stockman track-rode the mob at No. 3 Government Bore to prevent any more losses. Fred had come in with a drover the year before and did not return to 'Wave Hill'. Each day they took a water bottle and rode towards the north-west, where it was expected the bigger bullocks would stray. When beyond the outer circle of cattle tracks they split up and each rode a quarter circle back to the east-west stockroute road and returned to camp at the bore. Most of the country was open downs, but if they found cattle camped in the few timbered patches of country, they were given a start towards the water. After a while, it was only when light thunderstorms fell, that the cattle had any inclination to go further out. This job went on for four months, during which time Bill and Jack had gone off contract drilling.

During the summer of 1939 they had helped Dave Cahill put his small herd together and took them back to the 'Shandon Downs' yards for branding in the hope they would stay there. This was rather pointless, as they were no sooner let go than they returned to the sweeter flood-out country on 'Eva', which they now considered home.

Around 1920, Dave Cahill left copper ore-carting in the Cloncurry area to come to the Territory. He had camped in a tent and bough shed on the Leichhardt River with copper miners, Campbell and Mulharry, before they received recognition for their large silver, lead and zinc find. They were broke when Dave was camped with them and asked him to go into partnership with them, but the Irishman chose to move to the Barkly Tableland where he had a contract to build earth tanks for

Syd Peacock. After Campbell and Mulharry sold their claim, it was developed into the giant Mt. Isa Mines.

Dave's contract with Peacock for the construction of earth tanks on the Barkly Stockroute brought him several thousand pounds and with this he bought into a partnership with Jack Keiran on 'Seven Emus', east of Borroloola. He reckoned he wasted thirteen years of his life there before moving to 'Shandon Downs', about the same time as the Chambers moved to 'Eva'.

Dave had an Aboriginal couple working for him named Jim and Dolly Ross. Dolly was cook, housekeeper, washerwoman, headstockman, you name it. The station goat herd camped close beside the couple's tent fly and one night a pack of dingoes came in and attacked their big, white bull terrier-cross and a fierce fight raged right across their swag. The mob of goats cleared out and had to be tracked down the following day. Fortunately, Jimmy was an excellent tracker.

The big white dog frequently went off for a night out with the dingoes. He must have been a good fighter to avoid being killed by them. Of course the inevitable happened and a few white dingoes with small black patches started to make an appearance. Sid was a dog lover and always thought Snowy was a good type of dog and made a bit of a pet of him. After the dog's dingo progeny came on the scene, Sid thought he had better do something about it. Just on daybreak one day the dog put his front feet up on the old man's bed. In a flash Sid caught him and tied him securely, before calling Alf to hold the dogs hind legs while he castrated him. When the operation was over, the dog went straight home and never roamed again. When Dave Cahill called in to get the mail ten days later, Alf found it hard to keep a straight face when he said, "What do you know? Old Snowy went away fighting with the dingoes and they bit his balls clean out!"

Dolly had been employed by this old chap for thirty years. She came as the child bride of Cliff, a remarkable man who could turn his hand to anything on the station. When he died of pneumonia, it was a sad loss for Dave as well as for Dolly. Her present husband wasn't keen on work at all, but was an excellent horse-hunter and tracker. Old Dave always reckoned that if Dolly had testicles, she would be a bonza buck. Her home country was on the salt water at the mouth of the Wearyan River east of Borroloola. The old lady could remember as a small girl seeing Chinese prospectors coming back along the coast route into Queensland from the Halls Creek gold rush. One apparently became lost and was killed and eaten by the tribe. When asked if she had tasted any, she replied, "I been eatem one little piece, just like a pig."

Dave gave the Chambers 110 bullocks as payment for sinking the 'Shandon Downs' bore. The bullocks were bred at 'Seven Emus' down on the coast and bore the ITK brand so they were cross-branded with the newly acquired 'Eva' brand, JTJ. The boys had to hold them until they were sold to a Vestey's pastoral inspector and put in a travelling mob to Queensland. When the Vestey's pastoral inspector came to look at the young bullocks, he made a preliminary offer of two pounds ten shillings per head. Sid said that he would have to talk to the Missus. Lucy sent him back three times until he got the right price of three pounds ten shillings. This was a paltry sum, but buyers were scarce.

Dave was a good neighbour and a great character. Once, when Alf attended a 'Shandon Downs' muster, the old Irishman had two Aborigines and their wives helping out in the stock camp. The cattle were scattered everywhere in small mobs and there were no paddocks or fencing, just a few small yards scattered about where the mustered stock was yarded at night. Moving from yard to yard meant shifting camp.

The two women had a tame feral cat which had just recently had kittens. They were very fond of the mother and babies and didn't want to leave them behind when they shifted camp, so they decided to carry the kittens on horseback in a billy can, as they sometimes did with pups. All went well for a while until the billy can was handed to Dave, who commented, "Now ain't I a wasted husband?" He had been carrying them for a while, when one of the horses whinnied and frightened the kittens and one sprang out of the billy can and ran up the horse's mane to its ears. This made the horse duck its head so quickly that Dave, billy can and kittens were neatly thrown to the ground. Amid the confusion and the swearing the kittens took off into the long grass and were never seen again and that night the female cat cleared out too. "Good riddance," said Dave.

Dave was no rough rider. When he was on 'Seven Emus' with Bill Harney, he had a mare that got in foal to a drover's donkey jack. His Aboriginal stockmen broke in the foal and could ride it bare back and do anything with it. At the end of a very dry year Dave had to ride the boundary of a small paddock. His Aborigines had gone on walkabout and his horses were in a low condition so he said to Bill Harney, "I'll ride that mule today, those boys can do anything with it."

He saddled up and as he put a foot in the stirrup to mount, the little mule brought his hind hoof up and cow-kicked his foot. "If ye are gettin' on I'm gettin' off". He commented drily as he determinedly gathered up the reins and made a swing for the saddle. The little mule suddenly dived in under him and tipped him right over the saddle to land on the broad of his back with the reins still in his hands. Lying there he looked up at the animal and exclaimed, "Sure in faith the Good Lord was a poor judge of horse flesh the day he rode one of ye bastards!"

Passing drovers were given a list of cattle brands to look out for and pick up along the roads. A score or more drovers passed through 'Eva' each year. Most would never dream of taking any JTJ cattle on in their mob, but there were always a few that were unscrupulous. As a precaution the mobs of suspected passing drovers were inspected as they went through the property. One chap had stayed a week on his way out with his droving plant and used the station's yards to break in some horses. 'Eva' generously killed a beast to feed him and his men and he promised to return the favour on his way back. True to his word when he came back with his mob he said, "I have a nice big fat killer in the mob to kill tonight. Come down later to collect half." Alf arrived at his camp just as he had knocked and bled the beast and the drover said to him, "I hope this cow isn't yours. I picked her up at the bore back through the boundary." Sure enough it was one of theirs and Alf had no other option than to accept his own meat.

The pick-up request was much abused by ringers in station stock-camps and they got away with scores of cattle. Stock belonging to the big landholders was considered fair game, whereas mostly the small man's cattle were respected. It was a general rule that killers always belonged to someone else. After knocking a killer, the expression, "Let the good Lord provide", took on a different meaning and referred to the absentee cattle baron, Lord Vestey, whose herds provided the majority of killers.

During the latter part of 1939, the Reverend Goy from the Presbyterian-run Australian Inland Mission, called at 'Eva' a couple of times. He told Lucy that as soon as it could be arranged, a pedal radio set, produced by Alf Traeger in Adelaide, would be installed at the station.

At the end of November, Sid and Freddie took over the cattle-tracking, while the family went to Mt. Isa in the International. The road between Camooweal and Mt. Isa was just being sealed and there were small stretches of bitumen in evidence. Christmas was coming so Lucy took along a load of turkeys to sell. Another outlet for her poultry was Max Schoeber, the old German storekeeper at Newcastle Waters. He liked a few turkeys to put on his hotel menu, especially around Christmas. One year he asked a drover who was coming past 'Eva' with a truck to pick up half a dozen. The old truck gave up the ghost and the drover and his offsider spent several days trying to get it going. Inevitably they ran out of beef so they killed a couple of turkeys. In the end they had to walk away from the truck and the surviving turkeys gave the dingoes a good Christmas dinner.

While they were in Mt. Isa, the truck went in for repairs, the dentist was visited and the half yearly grocery order, which came by train from Townsville, was collected.

For the kids from the bush the highlight of the trip was going to the open air picture theatre. It was a far cry from the Brisbane city theatres they had visited in earlier years. The cinema served Mt. Isa well throughout the war and afterwards and a few funny stories circulated. Once, when a local Mt. Isa chap took a naive bush girl to see a wild west show, she disappeared when the shooting started. He found her crouching at his feet, terrified. She was hiding from the bullets being fired on the screen thinking that they would ricochet off the tin walls of the cinema and hit her!

Walking along the street in front of the paper shop one night, Alf chanced to overhear a young bush couple comment on the news headlines concerning "German Propaganda". The girl asked her partner, "Johnnie, what is the meaning of that big word — propaganda?"

To which he replied, "You see Maggie, it is like this. Now we're married, supposing I went away on a big long droving trip for twelve months and when I gets home, you have a little baby just born. You would be the goose, I would be the gander, but I would not be the proper gander, would I?"

The storms started soon after they got home, which made the new cattle more restless. 'Wave Hill' Fred decided he wanted to work where there were more Aboriginal mates. He went to work at 'Alexandria Downs' rather than return to his home at 'Wave Hill' where he had run foul of tribal elders. This left only Bill and Alf to do the track-riding. Flocks of magpie geese had started to arrive, which they often did ahead of the monsoon so the boys shifted their camp to a higher red ridge just before there was a deluge of eleven inches of rain. Next morning the Broad Creek was half a mile or more wide and the countryside was a quagmire, except for a few better-drained ironstone ridges. Track-riding became hopeless so they set out to ride the twelve miles home. This took the entire day and they arrived two days before Christmas. Now it remained to be seen how many cattle they could salvage after the wet.

Lonely years commenced for Lucy in 1940. Much of the time she only had the younger children for company. The menfolk were away attending musters and doing contract work, boring, tank-sinking and droving.

As predicted by Charlie Schultz, the bigger bullocks and dry cows took off in droves. Most of the cows with calves had been content to stay put. At best, a few may have gone as far as 'Beetaloo', where there was a good chance of getting them back. At the end of the mustering season a few stragglers, that had stopped with the first cattle they met at 'Beetaloo' and 'O.T.' cattle stations, were collected. The stronger cattle scattered further to runs such as 'Nutwood Downs', 'Hodgson Downs', 'Dunmarra', 'Tanumbrini', 'Elsey' and 'Roper Valley'. It was hopeless to try to recover any of them. They were a dead loss. Sid's only comment was, "We will just have to get more fencing done to avoid that sort of thing."

Sid wrote to Harry Bathern to find out just how many, if any had stopped among his herd. The letter took some time because the mail service depended on passing travellers. Max Schoeber, the general storekeeper/publican in 'Newcastle Waters', thirty miles from 'Beetaloo' passed on mail between the two stations. When the reply came, it was found that indeed some 'Eva' cattle had strayed to 'Beetaloo' and they reported that it had been a bad year for their own cattle drifting to the south-east. It was agreed that Alf should attend 'Anthony's Lagoon' and the 'Adder' block musters in order to collect their own and 'Beetaloo's' strayed cattle. Watty would then come over and help take the cattle home.

By the time Watty Bathern arrived with his team of four Aboriginal stockmen, Alf, working with the combined 'Anthony's Lagoon' and 'Brunette' stockcamps, had collected quite a few of the strays. Watty joined the camp at the Adder waterhole and because of his fear of death adders took extra precautions when rolling out his swag. This was partly because Jim Wilson had put the wind up him by spinning a yarn about losing a couple of horses to death adders just a few hundred yards from the camp. Watty rigged his bush net upside down, on top of his waterproof swag cover and put his blanket roll inside so that he had a three foot cheese cloth fence for protection. Brodie, the boss of the combined stockcamp and the manager of 'Anthony's Lagoon', said if self-preservation had anything to do with it, Watty would live to be a hundred.

Next day the 'Eva' and 'Beetaloo' cattle were drafted. Watty had sixty head to drive home. They spent the first night at a small yard on 'Eva' then collected more strays from the chain of flood-out lakes. The search for cattle through the bush involved riding over vast areas by day and because there were no yards, long hours watching at night.

Once back at 'Eva', Watty made his camp a couple of hundred yards over under a gidgee tree. He and his men had never seen pigs before and were fascinated with a mob of about a dozen roaming around. There was a lot of excitement when an old sow put her head inside their empty but greasy beef bucket and got it jammed. She charged off at a mad rate slap into a stub fence, which knocked the bucket off. There were five male suckers which badly needed castrating, so the opportunity was seized while there were extra men around who could run like emus. They thought it great sport and called it, "Cutting the bull pigs". During Alf's early days on 'Eva', Watty Bathern was a regular visitor to collect stray cattle and as he was always keen to help out in the mustering camps, he was given four or five pigs. Because of the wood shortage on the downs most of the large stations kept pigs to clean up any offal at the killing yards rather than burning it.

Sid learned a valuable lesson when he lost so many cattle and after that he decided to buy small mobs from the little men when and wherever he could. Sometimes they were mixed sexes, other times just steers, but he always made sure there was enough paddock room to contain them. The plan was quite profitable, particularly with steers that had come off inferior coastal land. After twelve months on the sweeter 'Eva' country they were fat and saleable. In the early years these small mobs were sold as killers to Tennant Creek and Mt. Isa butchers. By pooling their mobs, the small settlers shared the droving costs.

In April of 1940, Reverend Fred McKay arrived to install the long-awaited pedal radio. This linked 'Eva' to the outside world through the Royal Flying Doctor Service network. The transceiver was powered by pushing a set of bicycle pedals which generated an electric current. The most important advantages were that the Flying Doctor base at Alice Springs could be contacted in an emergency and telegrams be sent. The base operator at Alice had four sessions per day. At the beginning of these sessions he listened for any medical calls. During these times there was a doctor in attendance at the base, who prescribed first aid treatment from a medical chest with which all stations were supplied. If the case was serious, the Flying Doctor plane was despatched to pick up the patient.

Sid elected to do some yard-building with Tommy, an Aboriginal youth. They set up camp ten miles from the homestead on a good-sized waterhole. The alliance didn't last because the youth was lonely away from his tribal life and Sid's pace was too solid. The deaf old man had never worked much with indigenous people and he tried to learn some of their traditions from young Tommy. After a day or so, the lad got sick and tired of shouting back in answer to the barrage of questions and this resulted in an altercation. Sid never spoke of the incident but Tommy told the tale to another Aborigine and the story got back to the family. It was really quite amusing, although it could have had a more serious outcome for the old man.

Tommy explained, "This old man talk, talk all the time until I just properly knock up. Mouth can't talk anymore. Then that old man ask, 'Why you get sulky bugger?' So I hit him twice. He hardy old bugger. Can't fall down. Then he real quick hit me just like a horse kick, knock me down. I bin get up and run away. He bin yell out, 'Come back'. We shake hand and go to work."

Before the introduction of mechanical diggers and posthole borers, yard-building and fencing was certainly hard work, especially on the sunbaked, black soil. It was done using basic tools such as a crowbar, shovel and brace and bit. Sid's idea of fencing was the set five yards per panel, but the later introduction of star-shaped steel posts and the lengthening of the panels sped up production of the long fence lines and was much appreciated by the next generation. So determined was Sid to run sheep on 'Eva' that the first fence lines he built had posts long enough to carry six foot dog-netting, which he intended to install at a later date. For the time being he ran only three wires. The result, when looking along one of these fence lines, was somewhat like looking along a hedge. The posts were so crooked, it was hard pulling light plain wire through the holes and barbed wire had to be tied on the side.

Having experienced a few wet and dry seasons, Lucy and the lads were firmly convinced that Sid was on the wrong track thinking of making 'Eva' a sheep station. Over a few nips of rum with a land officer he had expressed this desire. This ambition played right into the hands of the big landholders who wanted to form a bullock depot and were looking for more downs country to add to the 'Cattle Creek' block, over which they had secured the grazing rights. This was the block next door to 'Eva', which Sid had taken up initially.

Alf went to 'Beetaloo' again late in 1940 to collect some 'Eva' cattle that had strayed and to buy more droving horses. By this time Harry, the old patriarch, was failing fast and complaining bitterly about the cooking. The quantity and variety of food had improved and now included onions, potatoes, jam and believe it or not, goat's butter. The old fellow complained of indigestion and blamed the food. "It's nourishment I need at my age, not punishment. I wouldn't have this trouble if I was to get good rich food, plenty of sponge cake, plum pudding and sweets. But what is the use? Paddy couldn't cook it, if I did buy the ingredients for him."

He then launched into stories of trying to get and keep supplies at 'Eva' in the early days and asked about the galvanised ship's tanks that were there. When station supplies came in once a year in the dry season, the tanks were put in the coolest place possible. Bags of flour were poured into them until they were almost full then a lighted wax candle was stood up on top of the flour and the tank sealed to make it air tight. Any insects were killed when the candle burnt all the oxygen inside the sealed unit and when opened eight to twelve months later, the contents would be free of weevils. Sometimes the containers were hidden from pilfering Aborigines by burying them.

Harry once stored a tea chest full of rice in a hut on the Adder Waterhole. That year there was a particularly bad plague of bush rats, so bad that at night-camps all the harness had to be suspended from tree to tree on a wire. When the sealed tea-chest was opened, he found a dozen or so dead and desiccated rats in the rice at one corner of the box. He said, "We just had to scoop out the smelly cake around them and thoroughly wash the remaining rice. We had to eat it or go hungry for months."

The grass rat, that seemed to come into that country in plague proportions every eight or ten years, was cooked in the coals and greatly relished by the indigenous people. They seemed to come from nowhere and for five or six months they overran the place making a vast network of small pads through the grass like cattle or sheep. Fox terriers just got sick of killing them and they popped beneath the wheels of motor cars. Like the lemmings of Northern Europe, they were there one week and gone the next, but unlike the lemmings, which are said to run over cliffs into the sea, these rats just vanished.

Alf often wondered about the heaps of stones that ran down the slopes off the ridge to the yards and lagoon on 'Betaloo'. It was evident that a lot of work went into gathering them. "How did you gather that stone?" Alf enquired.

"Well, rather than have horses crippling themselves on stones, I found a way. When I first come to the place, there was a fairly large tribal camp. When we killed, they liked to be given the offal and head of the beast to eat, so I set them to doing that job in exchange for it. If I thought they hadn't done a good job, I sprinkled a bit of flour from a perforated tin over the offal and told them it was poisoned, and had to be burnt. Next week they would work harder at the stone-picking job so as not to miss out."

Old 'Bulwaddy', one of the Territory's most colourful pioneers, died during the war years. 'Beetaloo' was left to his descendants. Wattie, who was uneducated, managed the property under the supervision of Elder Smiths and an Irish bookkeeper. The old patriarch once said that there were two things he distrusted — posh, white-collared office johnnies and Irishmen.

The frightened kitten sprang out of the billy can and ran up the horse's mane.

Dave Cahill attempts to ride the mule.

9.

Life on the Barkly Tablelands

Sometimes the men were away from the homestead for considerable periods. They didn't realise how much this worried Lucy until some years later. Olive once told Alf how their mother had drilled the children on what to do until the men returned, if something happened to her.

Being close to the stockroute meant that quite a few travellers passed by and some of them were dubious characters. One very hot day a foot-slogging swagman walked up to the house. He sought attention for his feet which were very swollen and blistered. His boots were dilapidated and he wore no socks which was the major cause of the problem. Lucy told him he should have been better prepared for such a long walk but cleaned his feet with saline and applied ointment to soothe the broken blisters.

About a hundred yards from the house he made a camp under a shady gidgee tree and remained there for five days and always turned up at meal times for his fill. After three days Lucy began to feel uneasy because the chap was hanging about too much and becoming a bit too familiar and he got very offended when she told him it was high time he was on his way. During the fourth night she was awakened by a rowdy clatter. Thinking the bagman was raiding the kitchen, Lucy woke Olive to come with her. She took a torch and the loaded twelve gauge shotgun and just as well it was only the cat because Lucy would have used that shotgun very accurately. Next day she offered him provisions for the road and told him to go and he reluctantly went on his way.

During the family's trip from Queensland to the Territory in 1938, the numbers of foot-slogging swaggies or bagmen diminished the further west they travelled but were replaced by scores of men with little horse outfits. Because of the long distances between properties the bagmen over the border were a totally different species. These truly independent characters wandered the country with a packhorse and several riding horses, taking on a little casual work when the opportunity arose.

As a result of living on their own they often had somewhat prickly natures and were familiar by nickname or reputation. Old 'Chungree' Crouch once travelled for a few days with another bagman, Fred Barr, who had a reputation for having a short fuse. When they arrived at a frequently favoured night-camp, Fred got off his horse and chewed several straws of grass then he said "No, we can't camp here. This grass is sour for horses. We'll have to go on further." "One way to be rid of me," Chung said. He stayed there and Fred went on.

A lot of the bagmen were very good stockmen, but most preferred to take on camp-cooking for drovers or musterers. Some were very good at the cast-iron oven culinary job as well as being pretty clean in the rough circumstances. Others were quite the opposite and gave rise to the saying, "He's far too greasy and dirty for ringing so he's taken on cooking."

'Piebald Jack' had a great reputation as a camp cook, but hygiene was not his strong point. Towards the twilight of his cooking days, his haemorrhoids were becoming troublesome. Once, after a good morning's branding, the ringers on 'Rocklands' station were given the afternoon off to clean up and do some washing. When that was done, all except Boy Bowman, who had an extra good western to read, sat around playing a few hands of cards. When the evening meal of rissoles was served up, everyone helped themselves to a generous serve and thought it strange when Boy insisted on having corned beef and bread instead. The next day he told the others, "If you had seen that old cow put his hand down inside the back of his trousers to push his piles back, then go back to rolling the rissoles without washing his hands, you wouldn't have eaten them either!" 'Piebald Jack' was given the D.C.M. by the head stockman. (Don't come Monday!)

Most of the bagmen had nicknames. 'The Sick Pelican' was a fellow by the name of Swan. 'Short Stop Turner' never stayed long at a job. 'The Sitting Shot' — the boss will never get a second shot at me. These western wonders were always much more respectful to lone station women than their southern counterparts.

Camp cooking wasn't always done by older men. Quite a few younger chaps took on the job to save a few extra quid to start out as boss drovers themselves. Most bosses agreed a good cook kept everyone happy and resulted in a smooth-running camp.

One yarn told about a bagman and the manager of 'Victoria River Downs' was very popular. A big bushfire raged over the station around Christmas one year, denuding the area of grass. The manager, Alf Martin, was very distressed when his breeding cows and calves lost condition and began dying in alarming numbers. At this time the station had about 170,000 branded cattle on the books and as many again unbranded. When Alf was discussing his woes with his men, an old packhorse bagman nearby tried to console him saying, "Never mind, Alf, my old packhorse died too; we stock owners have to expect losses".

Late in 1940 Sid learned that the iron from an old store house at Borroloola was for sale cheap. This coincided with the arrival in Borroloola of a coastal trading ship carrying their wet season's supplies and a Simplex windmill and pump from Townsville. Sid therefore decided to collect everything on the one trip.

The iron was used with fibro asbestos sheeting and flywire to build a fly proof dining-cum-school room and an adjacent store room. These were lined and sealed and a verandah was erected all round to make it cooler for Lucy and the girls in the hot weather. The floor was made of ant bed and covered with linoleum. This didn't last very long because of the termite problem. The small windmill with syphon pump was installed to pump water from the lagoon in the creek when it filled and saved hauling water in a forty-four gallon drum on the forked sleigh. When an overhead tank was installed, the area beneath it was concreted to make a shower to replace the bucket shower which gave only limited water. A cool shower at night was a great relief.

Bill drove the old International with Sid, Lucy and the family on board, to Borroloola. The truck was well-loaded on the return trip. Besides the supplies, iron, windmill and pump were several Aborigines. They were selected by Constable Ted Heathcote who was in charge of the Borroloola police station. Sid's intention was to establish a camp of Aborigines at 'Eva' as on surrounding stations, to overcome employment difficulties. Solitary Aboriginal employees got lonely for their own people and wouldn't stay long. It was thought that the women could help Lucy with domestic work while the men assisted on the run.

The trip took a full day and was long, hot and uncomfortable. The old chariot was very basic and the top speed was twenty miles per hour. It had a steering wheel, engine bonnet cover and radiator up in front and the only seating was on the boards of the carrying tray. Swags were the only concession to comfort and cushioned the ride a little.

At lunch time they pulled up and spent a couple of hours with the Darcy family at 'Mullapunyah Springs.' They had a magnificent garden with pawpaws, bananas and vegetables growing and producing prolifically. It was a pleasant change, after travelling through low, rough, spinifex-clad, ironstone ridge country, to wander through the several acres of lush garden. The soil was a rich, red self-mulching type and the whole area was watered from a spring. Lucy bought some fruit which they ate immediately because it wouldn't last the trip.

Mrs Darcy had selected this spot some twenty years previously. At that time her husband, George was a teamster hauling goods from Borroloola to 'Brunette Downs' and other Barkly properties. While their team horses were spelled during the wet because the roads were impassable, George and his wife did some copper-mining at nearby Kilgour Gorge. The miner's right entitled them to select a twenty-five square mile lease and when copper prices became unprofitable, they set up camp by the spring.

Mrs. Darcy was a typical pioneering woman with plenty of bush ability and boundless energy. The oasis was situated among stout old paper bark and eucalypt trees where the beautiful fresh spring water simply burst from the ground to be diverted into irrigation drains. In the garden there was a hole dug to make a thermal pool which provided a warm bath during the cold part of the year.

The Darcys were always over-supplied with fresh produce, so when the opportunity arose, they sold it to travellers. If George visited 'Anthony's Lagoon' or 'Brunette Downs' in his truck, he always took a load along to sell. The attractive stone buildings were situated beneath shady trees with water running by. Mrs. Darcy had made the mortar for the buildings by burning limestone in a homemade kiln.

There were thirteen children in the family. George bred horses and cattle but found it impossible to expand because no leases were being granted in the Territory at that time. The stock bred up and threatened to overrun their small holding. During the late 1940's leasehold land became available again and from the basis of a few milking cows and some horses, 'Mullapunyah Springs' developed into a station.

Towards the end of 1947, Mrs Darcy and her twelve year old son mysteriously disappeared and were thought to be lost. Thirty horsemen and Aboriginal trackers from surrounding stations scoured the country for a week and found no trace of them. Their disappearance was the subject of conjecture for many years and the riddle has never been solved.

The Aboriginal families were settled on 'Eva'. Peter had two wives, Darby and Sheila, who were sisters. Darby, the older woman, was well trained and a good worker. She had a child, Annie, about seven years old and another sister, Leila, about twelve. The other married couple were George and Maudie. He was a useful stockman, but his wife was in no way domesticated.

The big stations provided no accommodation for their Aboriginal workers, other than allowing them to build their own humpies. However, Sid decided to build them their own place. It consisted of a single room with an antbed floor, a verandah and an attached bough shed and had water piped to it. The building was not dissimilar to the Chambers' own quarters.

Building this accommodation proved impracticable. Peter's second wife Sheila, although a young woman, was very thin and experienced recurrent bouts of malarial fever. With the onset of the wet season, despite advice from the doctor over the radio each day and the appropriate medication, her condition deteriorated. Lucy tried to impress on Darby that Sheila should remain in bed because she had a high fever and could easily get a chill. Instead, when a strong wind sprang up, the older wife took the younger woman outside and poured water over her to 'kill the fire'. Sheila died very suddenly of pneumonia in the little house.

The police sergeant at 'Anthony's Lagoon' was notified, but was unable to come out because the road was impassable. He instructed that the burial be carried out forthwith. There was much wailing and mourning, and eventually a grave was dug. During some brief part of their lives, Sheila and Darby had attended a religious school so Lucy, Bible in hand, did her best to give Sheila a Christian burial. When the body was lowered into the grave, Peter, wailing in expression of his grief, grabbed up a blunt pick axe and raked himself down the skull with it, bringing forth a good flow of blood. "Killem my cobra," he cried repeatedly. Bill and Jack quickly gathered all the tools and only left a shovel for two other chaps to fill in the grave.

Corroboree mourning songs went on for the next few days, during which time they all shifted camp about a quarter of a mile away to grass thatched mia mias of their own construction. They refused to ever live in the little house again. Soon George and Maudie announced they wanted to join the 'Shandon Downs' work force because a tribal brother was employed there. This meant that Peter who was a good worker but inexperienced on a horse, was then called upon to try his hand at stock work. One day when he caught and saddled a quiet horse to go after a rogue milking cow he forgot to tighten the girth. The saddle went over the horse's head and as a result he broke his thigh. The Royal Flying Doctor Service was contacted on the transceiver but as there was no airstrip at 'Eva' the plane, piloted by Eddie Connellan, landed at 'Anthony's Lagoon'. The road was sufficiently dry for the policeman to drive the doctor and pilot out to the injured man.

The doctor took a look at Peter's leg and decided that it should be set before moving him. The sergeant was called upon to hold a mask of ether to Peter's face to put him out, while the doctor manipulated the leg. There was quite a bit of pulling and twisting and then the doctor took his boot off and placed his foot in Peter's crotch to stretch the leg back into place.

While all this was going on, Lucy prepared a cup of tea for everyone and instructed Darby to get ready to go with Peter to the Alice Springs hospital. Darby's two children were left behind in Lucy's care. Meanwhile Eddie Connellan inspected the well-drained ironstone ridge where the homestead and stock yards were situated. Though it was somewhat narrow and a bit short, he decided that an emergency airstrip could easily be fitted in, without going to a lot of trouble. The plane would have to run close by the house garden fence, but a strip would be useful for mail deliveries and in emergencies.

At night, the two young Aboriginal girls brought their swag under a small verandah off Lucy's room. After breakfast in the morning they did a few sweeping and cleaning chores and were then allowed to go off swimming or hunting around the lagoon or along the creek. Peter's leg mended readily and in two months the couple were returned by a medical plane coming to do a routine health check of station people in the area.

The family were glad to be reunited and live in their mia mia throughout the rest of the dry months. Their household was disrupted again, when Peter claimed Darby's youngest sister, Leila, as a second wife. His old wife was disgusted, but she had no recourse other than to make the matter known to the tribal elders at

Borroloola, and at the next wet season's tribal gathering there would be a big fight over the matter. Darby got on well with Lucy and was useful, whereas it was hard to find a job for Peter during the next few months. When they wanted to go off on walkabout at the approach of the wet, they were taken to 'Anthony's Lagoon' where they caught the mail truck to their coastal home. The little dwelling was subsequently used as a storeroom. Thereafter Aboriginal stockmen were employed casually on the station and there was never any attempt to make a permanent settlement on 'Eva' again. Alf learnt quite a lot about bush tucker and methods of hunting from these itinerant workers and from his visits to other stations, especially 'Beetaloo'.

On his last trip to that station he saw at least 500 pelicans on the big lagoons that were teaming with jew fish. The Aborigines watched the pelicans swimming up and down in formation. At a shallow end they reached down with their bills and easily captured the fish. The tribal people smartly copied this method and placed hollow coolibah logs in that end of the lagoon. When the pelicans had driven the fish towards the logs, they raced to the water's edge and stripped off their clothes to stuff the ends of the logs. Half a dozen helpers carried the logs out, which most times were full of fish. After immediate cooking in the hot ash of a fire the slightly charred skin was thrown away revealing the beautifully cooked flesh, which was eaten off the skeleton.

The same cooking method was used for flying foxes. Aborigines gathered them in quite big piles by throwing sticks into the daytime-sleeping colonies. Alf didn't fancy eating flying fox, but could see the logic of cooking them in their skins. The little creatures hung upside down from the branches of trees, resembling large black socks, passing excreta and urine all over one another in a distasteful and smelly manner. The whites who were game enough to eat them, claimed the flesh was delicious, like a good fat wild pigeon.

Alf also witnessed how the Aborigines on 'Beetaloo' caught budgerigars for eating. At the end of the dry season in some years, millions of budgerigars came in great clouds to water. The women employed two or three feet of twelve gauge steel wire to throw at the little birds as they rose from the water after drinking and fluttered for a few brief seconds. This often left as many as twenty or thirty crippled birds on top of the water to be gathered. The birds were then boiled feathers and all in a bucket of salty water and if the people were hungry enough, they didn't bother cleaning off the feathers. Sometimes the tribal people obtained flock pigeons in the same manner, but only when in plague proportions in exceptionally wet years.

After Peter and Darby left, 'Eva' was run almost entirely by the family. On the bigger established stations, there was always a tribal camp close by a permanent waterhole and these people had always been there and were content in their own environment. Among them there were smart stockmen able to hold their own with their white counterparts, but naturally enough there were a lot of aged people and children who were supported to get the cheap labour.

During the summer of 1941, good progress was made around the home area. There was a house, a good supply of lagoon water dammed up and a windmill pumping to the garden. The fly-proof dining room was working quite well. All the buildings were surrounded by a seven foot high netting poultry fence to contain the fowls and turkeys and extra horse paddocks had been added. There was a long stage between No. 2 and No. 3 stockroute bores. The area where a small back water caused by the damming of the lagoon extended onto the stockroute road had to be fenced in order to discourage drovers taking advantage of the water. The mobs of cattle would have polluted the household supply and made it unusable.

A well-defined, bypass road was made for the droving plants and travelling public to use and caused no difficulties until Joe Soiden, a drover who hadn't been that way for years, happened along with his wife, family and plant of horses. It was nine o'clock at night when the family heard the horse bells approaching and then an awful burst of abusive language. Sid and the two eldest boys were away at the time and Lucy went to investigate. Joe, with a whip over his shoulder and looking very surly, was near the front verandah when she intercepted him. He let fly with a veritable tirade of abuse, "Miserable sheep cockies, come out here stuffing up the country with their lousy wire fencing running illegally across stockroute roads. If I find my team horses torn by your barbed wire, I'll sue for damages. You people have no right putting a fence there at all."

Alf hurried to his mother's defence very quickly, saying, "We're sorry if your horses have been injured. Any decent drover would have worked out his day's travel and arrived in daylight to make night-camp, and seen the sign and the well-defined detour. Instead you came along moonlighting like a cattle duffer with something to hide."

The drover's response was vitriolic, "Come outside here, you cheeky young snipe, and say that. I'll give you a lesson in fisticuffs." Having heard of his reputation for being able to handle himself in a brawl, Alf decided not to test him out.

Lucy stepped in again and asked him to calm down, which he did and was given directions to a good waterhole and night-camp. He got away early next morning and Alf discovered the remains of a slaughtered beast on Broad Creek. As no other drovers had been through, he suspected that it may have been Joe Soiden having the last word.

When going out west with their plants, the drovers made a night-camp close by. If the 'Eva' boys were not too tired, out of sheer loneliness they would invite themselves over. They were always welcomed and enjoyed a few hour's yarning round their campfires.

In order to stop the spread of cattle tick, there were four cattle dips installed to treat Territory droving mobs moving east and south into Queensland. There were dips at 'Anthony's Lagoon' and Ranken River, Camooweal and 'Lake Nash'. The first two were controlled by resident police officers, acting as deputy stock-inspectors for the only Northern Territory veterinary officer and chief stock-inspector, Captain Bishop. He certainly had a big job trying to supervise all animal health throughout the region.

The only tickicide available at this time was arsenic. The cattle were driven through a deep plunge dip and had to swim a few yards before walking up a concrete-floored draining area. If the arsenic dip solution was too strong, it irritated their skin, caused hair-loss and a tendency to overheat. Because of the burning discomfort caused by the dip, even well broken-in bullocks, that could be easily night-watched by one man, required two. Drovers always dreaded the first night after a dipping. After the war, DDT, Rucide and organophosphate were used. They didn't have the same irritating effect on the cattle but were found to be residual poisons and were banned.

Towards the end of the 1940 droving season, the Northern Territory Police Force were having some difficulty with a certain constable. He was a single chap and said to have well connected relatives, so it was decided to give him another chance and send him out to 'Anthony's Lagoon'. This was considered a nice quiet place to get over his addiction problem.

In those days the officer in charge of remote police stations had a very wide range of duties such as protector of Aborigines, acting unofficial postmaster, commissioner of affidavits and unofficial stock inspector.

One of the first tasks the new constable performed was to charge the dip in readiness for the next mob of bullocks. A mob of 1,250 young shorthorn store-bullocks from 'Wave Hill' in charge of drover Charlie Huggins, was due through in a day or two. The young police officer read his book of instructions on how to charge a dip-vat with the arsenic dip. The arsenic was supplied by the Department in soap-like bars about two by three inches wide and roughly twelve to fifteen inches long. The required amount of arsenic was added to a forty gallon vat of water which was brought to the boil and stirred well, making a strong mixture. The two Aborigines helping him said that the dip solution was far stronger than that used by previous constables but he ignored them and charged the dip with a double-strength brew. Being a government dip, inexpensive test kits were supplied for the officers to use, but he didn't use one.

The old arsenic dip was cruel on cattle but it did kill ticks and provided that the mixture remained between point seven and point nine, the side effects soon settled. It was also simple to test the strength, using a test tube and common household ingredients in given quantities. When these ingredients were added to the dip mixture, the fluid changed colour and by pouring it into a glass-measure, the strength was easily read. Any stockman could do it. However, it was surprising how often old stockmen were just too lazy to do the test and claimed that they could tell by the smell when the dip was up-to-strength.

Around nine o'clock in the morning drover Charlie Huggins had his mob yarded for dipping. After a couple of hours, when over half the mob had been dipped, the treated cattle began to go mad. Three of the drover's men let them out of the yard and they rushed down and swam across the big lagoon. When the remainder were dipped, they did exactly the same thing after being let out. Drover Huggins suspected something was very wrong and before leaving the dip he took a sample of the dip contents in a beer bottle.

The only veterinary officer in the entire Northern Territory was called in to investigate the disaster at the 'Anthony's Lagoon' dip. Captain Bishop saw the dead and dying cattle and immediately took a dip-sample for reading. The result of this test was never disclosed, but rumour was that it was near double-strength. A pump was brought in to discharge half the dip's contents and then water added until the solution tested correctly. The drover's sample was confiscated and poured onto the ground.

The few hundred survivors were far too stressed to move on, so Huggins had to pay his men off and find agistment for his droving plant until the following season. The owners of the cattle, Western Grazing Company, could not pay out on an unfulfilled contract. Instead of going to southern Queensland and relaxing, as he usually did for the slack season, Huggins had to take casual work to survive. Naturally enough, Western Grazing Company claimed damages against the Government. The incident was hushed up, but unofficial sources estimated that they got a settlement of seven pounds per head, eighteen months later. This was presumably correct, as Huggins received a progress payment for the the completed 'Wave Hill' to 'Anthony's Lagoon' portion of the contract.

In March of the following year Alf attended a general muster of the area with the 'Anthony's Lagoon' stock camp. At least 500 carcasses lay within a 150 yard circle of the drover's night camp, mute evidence of the shocking event. So heavily impregnated were the hides with arsenic that they were unmolested by blowflies and weevils. Further out, beneath the coolibah trees where they had gone to seek shelter from the sun, were a dozen or more dead cattle under every tree. Only 360 live but still distressed 'Wave Hill' bullocks were mustered. All of these shorthorn bullocks showed evidence of bare patches on their hides where the arsenic had burnt their skin and they soon knocked up, tonguing with heat stress, when driven along at a slow pace.

It was surprising how the authorities managed to contain the story and prevent the media and the R.S.P.C.A. getting wind of it. The incident should never have happened. It was claimed by witnesses and those who saw the aftermath, as the most cruel mass murder of livestock in the Territory's history.

10

The War Effort

1942 commenced with a poor wet season and the war wasn't shaping up so well. The Northern Military Command thought that the enemy might attempt an invasion of the sparsely populated northern coast. Darwin had already been bombed heavily. One sortie of Jap bombers had even come inland and dropped half a dozen bombs on some large rocks just out of Katherine, mistakenly thinking them some sort of military installation.

All women and children residing north of a line from Tennant Creek to Camooweal were advised for their own safety to evacuate the area. Lucy made up her mind it would be much safer for her and the four younger children to return to her small farm 'Maroona', so the tenants were advised to move off. Sid appeared unconcerned about Lucy's imminent departure, commenting only that there was more remote bush up north to hide in from the enemy than there was down south.

Housekeeping and the difficulty of trying to supervise children doing grades two, four and six without the aid of a governess became too much for Lucy. Although the School of the Air had just commenced through the Alice Springs Flying Doctor Base, it was in its infancy and only offered a time slot of fifteen minutes to each grade. At least it encouraged children to speak to strange voices in the outside world. The mail service was still erratic and correspondence papers were often delayed.

Sid had quite a supply of .303 ammunition from the first World War and he decided that he should keep up his shooting practice. His favourite targets were the kite hawks that eagerly scavenged any scraps thrown to the chooks. As the hawks circled overhead Sid attempted to shoot them on the wing with the old Lee Enfield rifle. Every second or third shot was successful and on the strength of this he said that if a Jap plane did come over, he would at least be shooting back!

After one of these target-shooting sessions he had just walked inside the low iron-roofed shed near the kitchen window when a circling kite hawk retaliated by dropping a heavy bullock bone right above his head. Although very deaf, he

Boring plant and camp.

Horseback-drafting road bullocks for droving into Queensland.

"Hang on to her, boys!"

reacted with a startled jump, which sent Lucy and the two girls into gales of laughter.

Lucy and the four children left the homestead at the onset of the dry season. The place then became a bachelor establishment. The boys were often camped out on the run or away doing contract drilling, yard building etc. so eventually the wild dog population came in and ate all the poultry.

Bill Brodie had a white boar and three sows. The owner had sent them up from a farm he owned near Brisbane and the pigs soon learnt to cool off in the water trough at the station bore. They liked to sit on the float valve letting cool water from the bottom of the supply tank come up around them, sometimes to the extent of overflowing the trough into the paddock and wasting the precious water. They caused him so much trouble, he gave them to Sid. When the 'Eva' homestead lagoon dried up, Sid drove them the twelve miles to Surveyor's Water Hole. They lived off the land there quite contentedly and occasionally a crippled beast was destroyed for them to eat.

There were about 1,500 cattle and a couple of hundred horses running on the waterhole at the time. The rest of the herd was watering on a bore six miles further on near the main camp. One day Jack rode to Surveyor's Waterhole and found a beautiful unbroken filly that he admired, in a sad predicament. She had evidently been playing around at the waterhole and somehow got her foreleg wedged between a small, double-trunked coolibah. When the leg bled, the hungry pigs were attracted by the fresh blood and ate all the hide off the bone up to the knee. It was a deplorable and disgusting sight and Jack put the filly out of her misery without hesitation.

The season remained dry and with the large number of stock on the waterhole it was soon depleted. The pigs were shifted from their home of seven months and moved to a bore further on. To Sid's surprise, several days later when he checked Surveyor's to make sure there were no cattle or horses still there, he saw a pig of about nine months of age lying in the wet mud to keep cool. He wondered how on earth he had missed it. As he couldn't drive it or carry it on horseback, he decided to return next day and shoot it. When he came back the pig was gone. Two days later when checking the poultry water in the hen house at the homestead, he found the little pig lazing in the fowl's water! Amazingly, after a seven months absence this animal returned twelve miles to its birthplace and the only other water it had known in its short life.

The three boys took a contract to replace or drill three stockroute bores for the Northern Territory Works Department. The outside well-casing had rusted and fallen in on the old holes which had been sunk some twenty years previously. The increase in the number of travelling mobs put a lot of pressure on the bores. Over 60,000 head of cattle bound for Queensland came past 'Eva Downs' that year. Sid undertook to repair and clean out all the earth tanks and troughs on nine stockroute bores between 'Anthony's Lagoon' and 'Newcastle Waters'. This was to take place after all mobs had passed in October. It involved cleaning out and topping up bank heights in low places and using a scoop to push earth in alongside the troughs.

A lot of the tanks were full of dense bullrushes, sometimes nine or ten feet high, which harboured a good proportion of the king brown snake population. It was a case of grubbing bullrushes by hand with a mattock. They had to be hauled out before the horse-drawn silt scoops could go to work on the remaining black sludge.

The fifty feet square, old-style earth-tanks were originally constructed twenty years before by horse teams. The embankment walls were forty feet across the bottom and nine feet high and they could be filled to a depth of seven foot six inches and contained 180,000 gallons of water. In most cases the height of these earth structures had eroded and they now held a foot less water. Their maximum capacity was required to prevent a bottleneck of cattle. When there wasn't enough water at one bore, the mobs went on to the next and this bore would be required to supply two mobs and so on, causing much congestion and frustration at the watering points.

Drovers tried to maintain the weight of the cattle over the long journey so they liked to maintain a regular feeding and watering regime. The cattle were generally taken into water about mid-morning after they had a chance to eat the dry pasture. On the Barkly stockroute the troughs were of galvanised iron supported by iron frames. The troughs were made up of eight foot lengths, twenty-four inches wide and one foot deep. When they were joined together they measured something like 160-180 feet. This was filled from the earth-tank via a galvanized iron pipe controlled by a flood-gate.

Gangs of several men were required for routine maintenance of bores and windmills These men were stationed at Newcastle Waters township and were supervised by an engineering foreman. Provided there were no mishaps, windmills did an excellent job on the open downs, where there was plenty of wind. The mobile pumping-plant was seldom required to replenish the supply in the tanks.

In the early forties and due to the war the mobs of cattle being driven east into Queensland and down through the centre to South Australia increased. Smaller mobs of fat cattle also went to a small army abattoir at Manbulloo, out of Katherine. It was during this period that women started to appear in droving camps. One famous droving family was the Zigenbines. Charles Chauval made a movie called 'The Overlander' starring Daphne Campbell and Chips Rafferty which was based on the story of one of Edna's Zigenbine's epic droving trips.

Harry Zigenbine was a big man, tipping the scales at twenty stone or more. His wife and their three sons and daughters accompanied him on droving trips. Two of the girls, Edna and Kath, were excellent horsewomen and later took charge of mobs themselves when the old man became too sick to carry on. Edna carried out many droving contracts very successfully before her marriage. After that she took a job as common ranger with the Mt. Isa City Council in order to educate her children.

With three attractive daughters, old Harry always had plenty of young ringers in his camp, so he seldom had to do a turn night-watching. The young chaps seeking his daughters' hands would always volunteer to do it for him. One day Alf said to him, "Gee Harry, you must have a big wages bill to pay each week."

"Don't worry, I don't pay them. I even burnt some of their swags and they still won't leave."

Harry had a narrow escape once. He had just taken delivery of a mob of lively heifers from 'Avon Downs', which rushed every night going down the Georgina River. Once when riding a much valued mare, he had just turned the lead of the galloping mob when she hit a jagged limestone outcrop hidden in the long grass. Her skull was split almost clean in half, killing her instantly while Harry slid on over the top without a scratch.

Mrs Mackenzie was another female boss-drover. Her husband did the cooking while she did the droving. One trip she had a great battle keeping enough men in the team to handle the mob. Who should turn up when she was desperately shorthanded, with a packhorse, three riding horses and his swag but the old bagman Jack 'Chungree' Crouch. It was cold and windy and the lady, who wore leather jodhpurs, leather coat and a big black hat which didn't reveal much of her face, rode up to him and said, "Are you looking for work?"

"Yes."

"Have you had much cattle experience?"

"Only about thirty-five effing years, boy," was his gruff reply. Nevertheless he got the job and to his embarrassment found out later that he had been addressing a lady. Two days later another man got sick, a jackeroo pulled out, and the Aboriginal stockman was getting moody and longing to get back to 'Wave Hill'. Things were going from bad to worse. Mrs Mac then pleaded with old 'Chungree'. "Mr. Crouch, that blackfellow is likely to run away and leave us at any time. You will stick by us, won't you? You wouldn't leave just Charlie and me with this droving plant, truck and all these cattle would you?"

'Chungree' replied, "Look here Missus, I would leave you, if you never even had Charlie. You know me, I am not a man who is here today and gone tomorrow. I am here today and gone tonight." As it happened, he did leave shortly afterwards, but not before the company road boss, George McIntosh or "Million Mile Mac" as he was known, was able to get a couple of ringers to the camp.

A lot of bush characters had nicknames. "Million Mile Mac" got his from the hours he kept and the long distances he covered supervising some twenty-five or thirty Vestey travelling mobs from the Western Australian border down to Dajarra and Mount Isa rail terminals.

Mrs Stacey and Mrs Soudan were drover's wives who went on the road with their husbands and did the camp cooking as well as caring for a young family. It must have been a very hard life for these women, rising early to cook breakfast for the droving team, and preparing their saddlebag lunches of cold meat and bread, before waking and feeding the children. Then there was the washing up and packing the van to drive on to the next night camp. The interminable round of setting up and dismantling the camps must have been very tedious. When she arrived at the new camp she had to prepare enough food and cooked beef for both the evening meal and the following day. Later there were Mrs Charlton, Mrs Pankhurst, and Mrs Lewis cooking for their husbands in droving camps — all wonderful battling women. In wet weather they were sometimes left behind for a few days on their own with a bogged truck waiting for the ground to dry.

Often uneducated drovers were put in charge of valuable mobs of cattle. Brothers Hurtle and Elmore Lewis came from a family reared in a boundary rider's camp and had very little education. Alf once met the two brothers in Elliott, just prior to attending a wedding. They had a few beers under the belt and started to argue the toss. Eventually one threatened to sue the other for slander and defamation of character. "I would beat you in a court of law. I did have a little bit of education, I went to grade three before leaving school. You didn't go to school at all. You are too illegitimate to even sign your own name."

Later that day Alf attended the wedding held on a lawn beneath flowering poinciana trees. Everyone was dressed in their best and the male guests were decked out in light sports coats and ties. Just as the family photos were being taken, one of the Lewis brothers, well under the weather and dressed in shorts, singlet and high-heeled riding boots, parked himself beside the bride's mother!

Most drovers tried to reserve small waterholes along the track for horses and drinking water. Paddy Conway, a very bow-legged chap but an excellent cattleman and drover, had a mania about watering his cattle at any water available. Consequently he pushed his cattle onto small waterholes not used by others and became known as 'Puddling Paddy'. Once he was skiting in one of the Camooweal pubs about watering cattle, claiming his mobs were better watered than anyone's. This was too much for drover, Geo 'Hopalong Cassidy' Simmons, who had a short leg but was very stoutly built and well able to look after himself.

"You, water cattle against anyone in Australia! Why you couldn't water cattle at all. They call you 'Puddling Paddy', you couldn't water a mob of bullocks in Lake Eyre without giving it one hell of a stir!"

Although forty years older, off came Paddy's glasses. "I will have you know, young fellow, those are fighting words."

Ernie McCarthy was an extra good worker and was one of those ex-cooks who wished to start out as a boss drover. He worked at 'Eva' prior to putting together a droving plant to take delivery of a mob of bullocks from Western Grazing Company's depot, 'Helen Springs'.

The 1,300 head of aged, lean-gutted, long-horned, western-bred Shorthorns came to the depot the year before from perhaps a dozen or more places — 'Ord River', 'Limbunya', 'Willeroo', 'Mistake Creek', 'Manbulloo', 'Delamere', and 'Nutwood Downs', to mention a few. All these stations were renowned for having wild galloping cattle, consequently there were plenty of rogues in the mob to try out a newcomer. Ernie assumed the bullocks, having done a long trip the year before, were well broken in to the road. Things were fine for the first four nights. The fifth night he came through the 'Helen Springs' boundary fence onto 'Eva Downs', to what is referred to as Brady's Gap. The gap was where a north-south red spinifex ridge was broken by a small black soil plain. The inexperienced camp cook chose the night camp. It was surrounded by breakaway ground, which gave away under the horses hooves. Not a good place to camp with touchy, galloping bullocks such as this lot.

Something startled the mob during the night and the inevitable happened. The young chap on watch tried to ride flat-strap to swing the lead of the mad rush and his horse fell badly in a hole. The whole mob swung and passed close by the camp taking the two saddled and tethered night horses with them. The scrub was flattened by the mob as if a pair of bulldozers had dragged a scrub-pulling chain through a fifty yard wide strip.

Come daylight, all hands and the cook set about trying to round the mob up on the big plain to the east. Approaching sundown and after shooting two injured bullocks, Ernie calculated that he was 260 head short. He had found the tracks of the leaders heading straight out to the south east where they should have run into the flood-out area. Ernie intercepted a passing car coming from the west, and asked them to pass on a message to 'Eva'. When Alf got the message, he was just off to the 'Brunette Downs' races for a few days celebration. He and a young drover named Alan Hagan, who was breaking-in horses near the homestead, teamed up to give Ernie a hand searching for the lost cattle.

They rode directly to the big flood out area which covered twenty-seven square miles of country with water. When they skirted each side of the flood-out area, they found some of the missing bullocks on the western side and tracks of a fast moving mob heading south-east on the eastern side. It was estimated this mob was twenty hours ahead of them and therefore it was hopeless to try and catch them. That mob of seventy head was picked up eighty miles away by a 'Brunette Downs' stock camp a week or so later. Alan and Alf took the bullocks they had found to a nearby yard for the night and then parted company, Alan to a droving job and Alf, after letting Ernie know where to collect his bullocks, to the races.

During the many years that 'Eva' sold horses to drovers, there were a number of times cheques had to be presented a couple of times, but they all came good in the end. "Bad Paper Bill" had a reputation for passing dud cheques. During the war he had a man with him, an ex-miner nicknamed 'The Underground Stockman'. When the trip was completed, 'Underground' wished to board a plane for Brisbane to visit his old mother. Not wanting to be bothered with a worthless cheque, he asked to be paid in cash.

"I will give you a cheque," Bill replied. "You can take it along to the Army Quartermaster Store to cash it. They know you worked for me."

"No. Why don't you take the cheque along to them and get the money in cash for me?" 'Underground' asked.

"Oh no. I can't. They won't take my cheque," was Bill's reply.

Though some drovers had a reputation for taking horses, the Chambers only ever had two stolen. Once a black mare got away from Colin, but it returned to 'Eva's' western boundary gate where it was picked up by a drover who was on his way to Wyndham. He never really pinched her. As he said, "I only just took a loan of her to take a mob into Wyndham Meat Works." Alf met him at 'Newcastle Waters' on his return with another mob and he said, "I have a black mare of your brand. Would you know who owns her?"

Alf knew the number and had a suspicion the drover had her, because his had been the only droving-plant to go out west at the time the mare went missing.

"Would you sell her? She has out-worked any other two horses in my plant," he said.

Alf refused to sell her because she was an exceptional horse which never panicked in the sloppy bluebush swamps. With her long back and great strength, even when bogged to the girth, she pushed forward on her belly. The mare had previously not been named, but after her return she was called 'Wyndham' in recognition of her long trip.

The 'Eva'-bred horses had a fair amount of speed, plenty of cattle sense and were reliable night horses and shooting horses so there was a good market for them with drovers and buffalo shooters. Good night-horses were much valued by drovers because when riding at full speed after galloping mobs of cattle, their lives depended on them. Alf's friend, drover Frank Erl was killed instantly in 1940 whilst riding his best night-mare. He had a mob of 'Nutwood Downs' bullocks that rushed badly near Dunmarra. Riding flat-strap in the pitch-black night, he ran into an overhanging limb.

In 1943, the Northern Military Command decided it was high time there was a mounted light-horse patrol in readiness, in case the enemy attempted to land in the unoccupied Gulf region. At 'Newcastle Waters', 180 horses were selected from 1,100 horses mustered and trapped on the north Newcastle Waters hole.

Many of the animals were unbroken and some were unbranded brumbies with a fair number still entire. These colts and stallions were castrated and later broken in. There were even some with splits in the points of their ears. Thirty percent of the horses purchased were unbroken, so the word went out for a good horse breaker. Through the World War 1 Light-horse Brigade records they located the renowned horseman and ex-trooper Jack Dally. Jack and his family were brought over from 'Anthony's Lagoon' in an army truck and they set up camp on the outskirts of the small township. Each day, aided by three good Aboriginal stockmen, he worked at the station yards breaking in the animals.

Sixty broken horses had already been despatched and it was agreed the remainder would be done in two lots. They had to be quiet enough to enable a trooper to mount them with a military-type saddle, and carrying a 100 pound load of extra ammunition, camping gear etc. As each mob of sixty head was ready Jack and his men delivered them to Dunmarra on Frews Pond, one day's travel to the north. The horses were test-ridden on delivery by the horse-patrol soldiers and were always satisfactory. It had been anticipated that delivery day would see a lot of decked servicemen, but Jack was a wizard at his job.

On his return from World War I he had followed stockwork in western Queensland, mainly droving. As a boss drover he had a problem holding a team of men together and was always short-handed, so the stations were reluctant to give him a droving contract. His wandering ended for a period of time when he met and married Nellie Biondi at 'Anthony's Lagoon'. Nellie was reluctant to move far from her family and kept Jack there doing casual work until the job with the Army came up. After its completion the family moved to Camooweal and Mount Isa.

When Alf was in Jack's camp one day, they discussed how long periods of loneliness affected people. He related a story concerning his World War I Light Horse Brigade mate, Jim Wilson. Jim was a race rider of renown on southern Queensland country tracks. When he was disqualified for some misdeed, he gave the gallopers away to follow cattle work, at which he really excelled. Like Jack he couldn't tolerate a team of men for long, so when he was offered the caretaker's job looking after the 'Adder' block for 'Brunette Downs', he settled down for a dozen or so years while the job lasted. The Aboriginal couple, Camel Ned and his wife Topsy were his able assistants. In the dry season after waterholes had dried up, cattle were shifted on to the Adder Bore. Here Ned cut the cordwood into the right lengths while Jim stoked and attended the old steam engine which pumped the water. The wood was cut by a contractor who was paid per cord, a stack that measured six feet long by four feet high and four feet wide, and carted to a huge wood heap by the station horse team.

In the wet season, when Ned and Topsy joined other tribal people for the three or four months customary walkabout, Jim was entirely on his own. His nearest neighbour was at 'Anthony's Lagoon', some thirty miles away. With no roads and no means of transport but his horse, he only went in to collect his mail once a month. During this time he read many books, but without a radio it was a lonely life. He had often remarked to his mate Jack Dally, "Come out and stay for a week for a good yarn about old times." Jack, who had just broken in three young horses which required a bit of work, said to his wife, "I will take them out to Jim for a week. The thirty mile ride is just what they want and Jim, poor fellow, must be lonely."

The evening Jack arrived at Jim's camp, the two old mates talked beneath their mosquito nets long into the small hours of the morning. Jack woke at daylight to find Jim had gone, so he stoked the fire, put on the billy and made a small stew in the camp oven for breakfast. Jim returned riding bareback with all Jack's horses and said, "You are going this morning, aren't you Jack? I've brought your horses up for you."

When Jack arrived at 'Anthony's Lagoon' that afternoon, he said to his very surprised wife, "Nell, what else could I do? Jim had evidently talked himself out and wished me to go."

Tom Cole had shares in a couple of properties out of Pine Creek, 'Goodparla' and 'Esmerelda', from where he went buffalo shooting on the Wildman River country. His partner, Jack Guild, also had properties in the Pine Creek and Maranboy area. They were successful in drawing the ballot block 'Tandyidgee', an area of 1,100 square miles of country resumed from 'Newcastle Waters' station, and they urgently needed a bore. Two mobs of cattle had already arrived from the properties they had sold when they drew the better 'Tandyidgee' country. The combined herds were watering on Government stockroute bore No 6, about half-way between 'Eva Downs' and 'Newcastle Waters'. These cattle plus about 130 head of plant and breeding horses had the bore overstocked, so they had to hire a mobile pumping plant to keep up the supply of water.

Alf and Bill got the contract to sink the bore. Being wartime, a lot of things were rationed. Government coupons had to be produced when purchasing items such as tea, sugar, rice, petrol, clothing and blankets. To get enough petrol for the two trucks used to carry out contract work was quite difficult. There was certainly no joy-riding. The boys loaded the trucks with the plant and set out to Tom Cole's camp. Next morning after picking up some fresh beef, Tom showed them the new bore site, which was seven miles south of stockroute bore No. 7. Near this bore there was a United States Army transport staging-camp.

Being a friendly outspoken bushman, Tom quickly got to know several ex-Texan cowhands, who wished to come along for the ride and join Tom at his camp later. At lunch time their genial host offered them a traditional Aussie bush meal, rib bones and johnnie cakes. He set to work making the johnnie cakes then threw them on the hot coals to cook with the rib bones. He boasted that this was top Australian stockmen's tucker. One amazed Yank remarked, "Tom, who is going to eat it now that you've dropped it all in the God-damned ashes?"

Tom, no doubt, was trying to show how Australians did things in the raw. Tom, Alf and Bill hopped into the tucker, but the Yanks only took a couple of bites and declared, "No thank you, Tom, no more rib." The 'Eva' boys thought they were just too well fed. By this time they had heard Tom utter his favourite saying, "Hell West and Crooked". His book of that title later became a best-seller.

The bore proved difficult to drill and they had all sorts of problems, added to which Alf lost his hat down the hole and no amount of fishing could retrieve it. He had found an Australian Army steel helmet minus the inner band lying by the roadside, so he wore that to provide some protection from the sun. With every jolting bump of the truck on the rough roads its weight banged on top of his head with a resounding clunk.

Good rain throughout the district ran a few small creeks and indicated an early start to the wet season. A chain of waterholes filled along Tandyidgee Creek that would last seven or eight months and provide water for Tom's herd so he thought the boys should get home while they still could. They planned to return in April of the following year to complete the job.

As Tom didn't have a vehicle, before they left he asked if they would use the truck to haul a quantity of posts he had cut for yards. The boys were happy to do the job but weren't able to get enough petrol. "No worry, I have plenty of petrol for you. Matter of fact I will pay you with half a dozen drums of fuel."

That night was bright moonlight, so Tom said he would load them up with petrol. As they approached the U.S. Army Staging Camp he told them to switch off the truck lights and take a rarely used bush track across country for about a mile to a spot where they found twenty-five 44 gallon drums lying on their sides.

"I don't want anyone to know where I have this hideout, so it's best to come in darkness," was Tom's only comment. Being desperately short of petrol, the boys asked no questions but were left in little doubt that "Uncle Sam" was their unwitting benefactor.

Half-way home two of the old tyres on the truck blew out and they didn't know what to do. Bill had a brainwave. On the back was a quantity of cement and blue metal that had been discarded at a U.S. rubbish dump. Bill thought that if this old relic had once run on solid rubber wheels, why not fill the tyres already on a rim, with a mix of concrete then slide a large sleeve inside the rupture and leave it all night to set. They did just that. Next morning they put one on and kept the other as a spare. It took some loading. All went well on the damp black soil but when they hit a mile of hard country the concrete began to disintegrate and escape from the rupture. The spare concrete wheel was fitted and it lasted for the last twenty miles home. A new set of tyres was definitely needed after the wet.

The unfinished bore was left in limbo as a result of the big 'Tandyidgee' cattle-duffing case after which the property was sold. The new owner didn't want a new bore, so the boys put their hard work down to experience — a 290 feet deep posthole.

11.

The Great Cattle–Duffing Case

The Northern Territory beef barons had established their big runs where there was reasonable pasture and plenty of natural waterholes. The potential of country which was well grassed but without sufficient surface water was overlooked. This was the land that Sid selected in 1935, when cattle prices were low and in the midst of a nationwide depression. When the financial climate improved and bores could provide a good supply of sub-artesian water, the cattle barons resented the small farmers who had taken up the unoccupied land on their borders. With no fences the big graziers knew that the many unbranded calves in their poorly managed herds would be tempting to their less affluent neighbours, to whom they scathingly referred as 'cockies' and 'poddy dodgers'.

A couple of old timers, 'Bulwaddy' Harry Bathern and Davie Cahill, often warned the Chambers, "This is Big Man's Country. If they want it, they will try to kick you off." Davie Cahill was a true Irishman and 'agin the Guvmint'. He refused to fill in his postal vote at election time, commenting, "Never voted in my life. It doesn't matter who you vote for, the same old policeman will boss the country." In those days there was only one elected politician, Jock Nelson, to represent the Territory and the police wore many hats in the outlying areas.

On the recommendation of the Payne Fletcher Land Commission, 'Tandyidgee' was cut off 'Newcastle Waters' for small land-settler development. This was essentially because the absentee land owners, Lewis and Company, had done nothing to develop the big stretch of excellent grazing land. Tom Cole and Jack Guild were successful in balloting for it. Vesteys decided shortly afterwards that they urgently required a cattle depot half-way between their western empire and the fattening depots in Queensland. They selected the vacant block 'Monmonah' between 'Eva' and 'Tandyidgee', along the Barkly stock-route. A while before this, a land officer had tried to talk Sid into shifting to a sheep property down near the South Australian border but Lucy and the family were against it. Vestey's next move was to make an offer to purchase 'Eva', but the family refused to sell. With all legitimate efforts exhausted, the game then started to get rough.

When Guild and Cole were caught redhanded after a daring, large-scale cattle-duffing operation, the big boys saw their chance of discrediting and getting rid of the Chambers, so they could take over 'Eva'.

A combined race meeting and a farewell to the American troops who were departing from No. 7 Bore staging camp was held at Elliott on New Year's Day. Elliott was then only a large Australian Army staging camp. Tom Cole played the grand squatter with a couple of races horses, fraternising with the big brass. His ulterior motive was to spy on the 'Newcastle Waters' stockmen's immediate and future movements, while just a few miles away a daring cattle-duffing operation was in progress. Cole's partner Jack Guild, with the aid of one ringer and four Aboriginal stockmen mustered along the big Longreach water-hole on Newcastle Creek through to Lake Woods.

When the coast was clear, Tom Cole joined the musterers for cattle-drafting in readiness for the droving trip to Tennant Creek. While en route they picked up additional bullocks off the top end of 'Helen Springs'. In all, they collected some 500 head of bullocks bearing the wine glass brand of 'Newcastle Waters' and the BTA brand of 'Helen Springs'. The cattle were destined for the Tennant Creek butcher, Darkie Allan's paddock at Phillips Creek, twenty miles north of the town.

With two of the stockmen and the white ringer Tom took the mob over the north-south bitumen road onto the Overland Telegraph line, which they followed as their stockroute. Tom had been employed as a linesman along this stretch some twenty years before, using camels, and knew the country well. In order not to be observed he had made sure that all the 'Banka Banka' Aborigines were out east on walkabout. The plan came unstuck when the mob was spotted by some aged 'Helen Springs' Aboriginal people, on walkabout. They thought it strange to see a mob of cattle being driven south at that time of the year and reported it to the elderly Bohning's at 'Helen Springs'.

Straightaway old Jack Bohning was suspicious and had his stockmen get a plant of horses together to track-ride a couple of his northern bores. They soon discovered where cattle had been mustered and held together on a camp for drafting. The trail leading over the bitumen road and onto the Overland Telegraph line was obvious because the cattle had been moved in light rain. Jack reported the matter to the 'Newcastle Waters' police. Police horses were mustered and Aboriginal police trackers were quickly put on the tracks. The trail to the butcher's paddock was easy to follow and there they found the big mob of freshly released cattle. The police were so close on the duffers' heels that Cole's white ringer and two Aboriginal stockmen would have run head on into the police patrol, if they hadn't unwittingly taken a short cut around the opposite side of a hill and made a clean getaway.

Tom Cole had collected from the butcher and got clear as soon as the work was done. He soon learned from his cockatoo mate in 'Newcastle Waters' that the police were on his trail. As soon as the two Aboriginal stockmen caught up with him, he secured a fresh plant of horses and headed for the safety of the so-called Underworld, over the Western Australian border. Tom was on the run and this was a popular destination for wanted men and petty criminals in those days.

He knew all the western roads like the palm of his hand and all the head stockmen manning the outstation stock camps were his mates. He had no problem getting fresh horses, but the police following his tracks weren't so fortunate. The two Aborigines remained at Pidgeon Hole, an outstation of Victoria River Downs. Tom tried unsuccessfully to bribe them into changing their names. That was a futile exercise because they had nothing to lose and the local tribe would soon tell the trackers who they were. Nevertheless, Tom made a clean getaway, sold his horses and gear in Halls Creek and boarded a plane for Perth.

Earlier in the previous year when droving his cattle to 'Tandyidgee', Tom ran foul of a ne'er-do-well ringer-cum-bagman. Tom employed him because he was very short-handed but the bloke was workshy. An altercation took place and the man was sacked. Vowing his revenge, he left his three or four horses at 'Newcastle Waters' and went to work on 'Eva', where he soon showed his true colours and was sacked again.

Following the Elliott races the ringer picked up his horses and arrived at Jack Guild's camp on No. 6 Bore, several days later. Guild was out stock-riding when he arrived, so he pumped the two remaining Aboriginal stockmen regarding Guild and Cole's whereabouts. They said that Guild would return that night but Tom Cole had gone east to steal cattle. The ringer saw his chance to get even when he surmised Tom had gone out to 'Anthony's Lagoon' and 'Brunette Downs' country after cattle.

The ringer rode east and arrived at 'Eva' next day and found only Jack and Alf at home. They had just completed a big horse muster for foal-branding and their tired horses were in the small horse paddock nearby. The bloke threw off his pack and swag and went in to dine with the brothers. He soon asked, "Where is Tom Cole? He came this way — nuggetting. You fellows have been with him doing a raid. I saw the tired horses in the paddock. Where is your old man and Bill now?"

They told him that the horses were tired because they had been mustering horses and that Sid and Bill were cleaning out the earth tank at No. 1 bore. The ringer didn't believe them and said that Guild's Aboriginal stockman had told him which way Tom had gone pinching cattle. He was determined to report the matter to the 'Anthony's Lagoon' station manager and the police. Next morning he set off early to do his pimping.

At No. 1 bore he stopped for lunch with Sid and Bill. When he arrived at the police station at 'Anthony's Lagoon', the policeman was away investigating another cattle-duffing incident. Bill Brodie, the 'Anthony's Lagoon' station manager and Jim Wilson, the overseer of the 'Brunette' outstation 'Adder' block, decided to investigate the ringer's accusations. Taking the informant with them as camp cook they rode along the stockroute through 'Eva' and 'Monmonah', the vacant block recently taken up by Vesteys, looking for any signs that Cole may have taken stolen cattle back. Their team of five or six Aboriginal trackers, who skirted several miles each side of the stockroute road, found absolutely nothing.

The search party passed 'Eva Downs' at night and their camp fire was noticed from the homestead, a mile or so over to the north-east. The next day, Jack and Alf saw their tracks and assumed that they were made by a drover's plant. The search was terminated after dark at Monmonah waterhole, eighteen miles from Guild and Cole's camp.

It was not surprising that the party chose to camp so far from Guild and Cole's camp. No doubt, the informer knew of Tom's reputation as a buffalo and crocodile shooter in the Top End and that he always carried an ex-German army long-barreled revolver. He was a crack shot and could bring down dingoes at sixty or seventy yards.

That night a severe electrical storm struck and the following day the unsuccessful search party returned to 'Anthony's Lagoon'. By riding long stages it only took a couple of days. Three days later Jack and Alf noticed crows and hawks hovering in the distance. On investigation they found two dead horses, lying back to back, only a hundred yards from where the party had camped. The 'Eva' horses were all inside paddocks so the dead horses had to have belonged to someone else. It was impossible to investigate the brands because of the advanced state of decomposition of the bodies. They were mystified as to who had camped there but came to the conclusion that the horses had been struck dead by lightning during the electrical storm.

One morning shortly afterwards, just as Jack and Alf had finished breakfast and were going off to the yards to break some young horses, Bill Brodie and Jim Wilson rode up. Jim was quite talkative and in an amiable mood. Brodie was sullen, which was not unusual. They said that they had heard that Tom Cole had been in the country recently and they had been out trying to track him down, but they didn't mention the dead horses. Brodie and Wilson then asked Jack and Alf if they had been with Tom Cole! They were shocked and realised immediately that they were acting on the informer's information.

Jack and Alf were camped out on Surveyor's Waterhole building a wire bronco yard a few days later when the policeman rode up. He interrogated them closely about their recent whereabouts and then ordered them to attend a police muster of 'Eva' and 'Shandon Downs' cattle in two day's time. Using Surveyor's Hole as the central point, the muster took place for about twelve miles along Broad Creek where the herds of both properties were running at the time. The police patrol team of fifteen horses and two trackers were joined by 'Brunette Downs' No. 2 stock camp. That was lead by Tom Barnes, the 'Brunette' manager with a plant of fifty horses, Jim Wilson from the 'Adder' block, a head stockman, cook and eight Aboriginal stockmen. Then Bill Brodie arrived with fifty or sixty horses and the 'Anthony's Lagoon' stock camp of twelve to fourteen men. Even Arthur Wilson, manager of 'Newcastle Waters', was persuaded to send his stock camp 120 miles with another twelve to fourteen men under head stockman, Joe Dowling.

The big muster revealed a dozen or so COT branded 'Anthony's Lagoon' cattle and 'Brunette Downs' BDT branded cattle, which were the normal wanderings from next door's unfenced 'Adder' block. They were cut out and into these they cut seven or eight yearling animals branded the previous year by 'Eva' and 'Shandon Downs'. The small mob was then tailed around by several stockmen.

When no 'Newcastle Waters' cattle were found, the manager was disgusted at having to undertake a round trip of 240 miles for absolutely no gain and called the muster a big waste of time and man-hours. Their head stockman smartly pulled his camp out. No doubt it looked impressive having some fifty odd riders in a police muster.

The police had given no indication of their intentions and eventually it all got too much for Sid, who went to their camp to order them off. "Now you have had your look and found nothing out of order I would like you to pack up and get to hell off my place. I can't have you fellows polluting this waterhole by using the lignum bushes around it as a lavatory." In the open downs country it was the only place to get any privacy. Not content with this, Sid then called Bill Brodie, whom he had thought a friend, a cur and wanted to fight him. At this point the police officer arrested Sid for obstructing a police muster and using abusive language to a police officer. This charge was never brought to court.

The police expected and hoped Bill, Jack and Alf would react violently to Sid's arrest and when they didn't, they were lined up with Dave Cahill and arrested on a charge of cattle-stealing — a very grave charge indeed. Straightaway, seven of the yearlings were shot and skinned. Five bore the 'Eva' JTJ brand, and two bore Dave Cahill's ATX brand.

The police seemed to think that if the lads were guilty, they would eventually confess if they put enough pressure on them. They were bundled into a truck for 'Anthony's Lagoon' where that night they made a formal appearance before a local Justice of the Peace and were committed for trial at the Alice Springs Magistrate's Court in three day's time. Sid was locked up in the watch house and the others were allowed to camp in their swags in the police backyard. The next day they travelled by truck with the prospective Aboriginal witnesses and the salted cow hides, bound for Alice Springs. After a long day they were yarded for the night at Barrow Creek and proceeded to Alice Springs the following day.

At Alice Springs the boys were drafted into separate cells for a day and a half in the hope of destroying their morale before their appearance in the Magistrate's

Court. At last, after four dusty days the prisoners washed their clothes and had a bath. The gaol governor was a jovial ex-policeman by the name of Muldoon. He was quite pleasant to his new guests and said, "Don't worry boys I've spent eight years in this gaol and it hasn't hurt me." Nonetheless, being confined with convicted criminals was a humiliating and demoralising experience for the innocent boys from the bush. It appeared that the stay in gaol was planned by the prosecutor who knew exactly when they would arrive but failed to arrange an earlier hearing in the Magistrate's Court. Alf suspected that isolating them in cells like common criminals was all part of the softening up process.

By comparison, Jack Guild and Darkie Allan, who were arrested by the police officer at 'Newcastle Waters', had their case conducted before a Magistrate immediately upon their arrival in Alice Springs. They were released on bail with the proviso that they reported each morning to the police station. No stay in prison for them.

The Magistrate committed the case for trial in the Supreme Court and the prisoners were finally released on bail, which they paid themselves. Once out, they set about the task of securing a good lawyer and settled on Mr Travers, who was a King's Council from Adelaide. This put the cat among the pigeons because the prosecuting party assumed that they wouldn't have the money to pay such a highly qualified mouth-piece.

During the five or six days before their case came up, the 'Eva' boys occupied their time watching the trial of Bill Caine, a fellow inmate of the Alice Springs gaol. Caine had been caught redhanded cattle-duffing by the same 'Anthony's Lagoon' police officer who had charged the Chambers. When the saga leading up to the Chambers being charged took place, that officer was out on the Nicholson River above 'Alexandria Downs' chasing Caine. The duffer was caught with freshly branded calves in his possession which he had stolen from 'Alexandria Downs'. Caine had left tracks all the way to his own station yards for the police trackers to follow. He subsequently branded the calves but when they were put together with 'Alexandria' cows, they soon showed where they belonged. With his own men corroborating the evidence, a guilty verdict was inevitable and resulted in a six month sentence.

Because the Caines case was so easily won, the police officer and Tom Barnes thought they could use the same tactics to win the case against the Chambers. If the Aboriginal stockmen from 'Anthony's Lagoon' and the 'Adder' block swore to have seen the slaughtered yearlings as calves on their 'Brunette Downs' or 'Anthony's Lagoon' mothers some eight or nine months previously, they would get a conviction. If they won their cooked-up case, it would break the Chambers and force them to sell 'Eva'.

Jack Guild had to report to the Alice Springs police station each morning while he was out on bail and he kept his eyes open. During the few days prior to the Chambers' case coming to court, Tom Barnes and Bill Brodie were observed several times laying out the cow hides on the ground in the back yard of the police station. The Aboriginal stockmen, who were the star witnesses, were schooled to say they had seen the beast, from which each hide came, suckling a 'Brunette Downs' or 'Anthony's Lagoon' cow the previous year.

When the big day in court arrived and these Aborigines were put in the witness box, they reeled off parrot-like the evidence they had been taught to give. They knew them all right, little calf on this cow and that cow. When the King's Counsel cross-examined them, in their mind he was just another "big fellow boss". They would tell the truth to him if he asked them the right question.

He said, "Now, who told you that you would have to remember what calf this hide came from?"

All the Aboriginal witnesses then naively incriminated the 'Brunette Downs' and 'Anthony's Lagoon' managers, saying, "Mr Barnes and Mr Brodie, they tell us each morning behind the police station." The learned man went on with more questions.

In the end he asked them, "When did you first set eyes on this beast?"

They answered, "Just before it was shot to take the hide."

Travers continued, "Then in actual fact, you had never seen it before at all?"

"That is right," they replied.

At a complete loss as to who was who, or just what was to be presented as evidence, these Aboriginal stockmen simply told the truth and made a mockery of the cooked-up case. Under cross-examination, Jack said the hides were just normal shorthorn cattle colours and had nothing whatsoever to distinguish them. If one or other of them had some unusual marking such as a green spot, one might be able to remember it. Dave Cahill gave a good account of his whereabouts when the crime was said to have been committed. He said in his broad Irish brogue, "I was away out to the north of my country looking for a supposed waterhole with my two Aboriginal stockmen. It was real virgin country."

"Just what do you mean by real virgin country, Mr Cahill?" the judge asked.

His typically Irish reply was, "Real virgin country where the hand of man has never set foot." This was corroborated by his two Aboriginal stockmen.

Summing up, the Judge said in his opinion the station managers were dangerous, unreliable witnesses and lucky not to be charged with perjury. He found that there was no theft committed by any of the men charged and they were acquitted. The Chambers discussed the subject of compensation for wrongful arrest with the King's Counsel but he said the case would have to be referred to the Privy Council in England and would cost a mint, so they didn't proceed with it.

The 'Tandyidgee' case proceeded promptly thereafter and Guild and the Tennant Creek butcher were also defended by Mr. Travers. The 'Eva' boys had to wait a couple of days to get a lift to Elliott, so they passed the time listening to the court proceedings. The evidence compiled by the prosecution was increasingly incriminating and the judge found them guilty. He imposed a six year gaol term or a fine of 6,000 pounds each upon Guild and Darkie Allan — a lot of money in those days. The Judge remarked, "The country is at war and needs the money more than men in gaol." Larry Sloan, the stockman who assisted Tom Cole on the droving trip to Tennant Creek, was released on a good behaviour bond for a period of eighteen months.

Sloan and the three 'Eva' lads were marched off to the recruitment office to be conscripted into the army. When Mr. Travers heard this, he consulted with the officers of the Northern Territory Military Command. It was decided that the lads were more desperately needed as manpower on the stations to keep up the supplies of beef and to move livestock in the face of invasion, than as cannon fodder.

Following the cattle duffing case, Bill Brodie, manager of 'Anthony's Lagoon', and Tom Barnes, manager of 'Brunette', didn't last long in the area. Brodie moved to Charters Towers where he was killed in a motor accident. Tom Barnes took a job with the British Food Corporation in Queensland and his position on 'Brunette' was taken by his brother Eric. The two were as different as chalk and cheese. Eric was always willing to assist the small landholders and was a great friend to all.

The attempt by the big landholders to evict the small men on the downs country failed. After the war, a new lands officer, Gordon Buchanan, a grandson of that grand old man Nat Buchanan, was appointed along with Dan McInnes. Their job was to encourage practical cattlemen to ballot for blocks of land in order to clean up the great herds of feral cattle and bring the country into better production.

During the next year, the elderly Bohning couple on 'Helen Springs' failed to lure their sons back to run the property, so they decided to sell. Land values in the Northern Territory at the time were nil and a book branding value of three pounds per head for an estimated five thousand cattle was put on the place. Western Grazing Company smartly snapped it up to add to their 'Monmonah' block for a spelling depot.

A station manager was appointed to run the place and prepare for the estimated 35,000 - 40,000 head of cattle that would come from the company's western runs. Stock yards and fences were erected in readiness and extra bores were sunk to provide more water. In the dry season of 1944, a good-sized mob of bullocks were put together off the property, to walk into Queensland for sale. Their sale value more than paid for the walk-in, walk-out price of 15,000 pounds paid for 'Helen Springs'.

A month or so after the cattle cases, detectives arrested Private T. E. Cole in Adelaide. He had only been in the army a very short time. The Northern Territory police escorted him back to Alice Springs to stand trial for cattle stealing, but a medical examination revealed that he was suffering from leprosy. The leper hospital on an island off the coast of Darwin had been bombed by the Japanese and was abandoned, so Tom was sent to St. Helena Island, Queensland's leprosy colony. It was the closest facility where he could be detained for treatment. He was bored and unhappy there and a couple of times he attempted to swim ashore through shark-infested waters, but was caught and returned to the island. After six months he was examined again and found to be quite free of the disease and was allowed to rejoin his army unit which was then in New Guinea, where he was to do service for the remainder of the war. This experience opened up new opportunities for Tom and he returned there after the war to shoot crocs for the skin trade and to start a coffee plantation.

During the remainder of 1943, the Chambers completed cleaning out and repairing stockroute watering points. At No. 6 Bore they met Jack Guild pumping water and caring for the 'Tandyidgee' herd. Jack had negotiated the sale of the property to Ted Low of Quorn, South Australia, who had previously owned 'Mataranka'. The terms of sale dictated that Jack mind the cattle until after the wet season when Low's drover would come up from South Australia. Low's son Rex was to help Jack muster the herd for the trip down over the state border to Rex's 'Dalhousie' station. 'Tandyidgee' was then rented to 'Newcastle Waters', who had leased it before Cole and Guild won the ballot. As it turned out, the sale to Low was only a front for the owners of 'Newcastle Waters' to regain possession of 'Tandyidgee'. Following the March muster Guild left the Northern Territory to follow stock work in western Queensland.

Alf tried to keep downwind of the animal and concealed himself behind the sparse timber.

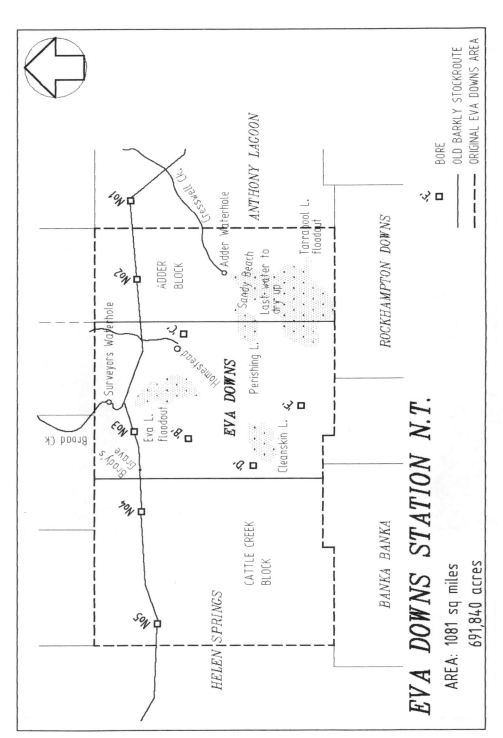

EVA DOWNS STATION N.T.

AREA: 1081 sq miles
691,840 acres

Detail of 'Eva Downs'.

Part Three

Triumph of the Battlers

12.

The Flood-Out Country

After World War II the Northern Territory fully emerged from the nineteenth century. Improved roads enabled a much wider use of motor transport and horse teams gave way to machines. The advance in communications technology and the aeroplane contributed to a period of rapid growth and development unseen in the Territory since the first heady days of pastoral settlement in the 1880's. The Northern Territory Administration, realising that smaller landholders tended to run their operations more efficiently and productively, started encouraging small settlers to take up land. Blocks of land were split off some large pastoral properties and balloted to small settlers.

At Christmas 1945, Jack had his first holiday south. He had been in the Territory continuously since he arrived on 'Eva Downs' in 1938. At Mungallala he met and courted his future wife Dulcie Rice, of Manangatang, who was there holidaying with relatives.

A number of years previously the pilot, Eddie Connellan, saw the potential for an all-weather airstrip on the well drained ironstone ridge where the mud house was built. The position of the house restricted the size of the strip. Towards the latter half of 1947, Jack was about to be married and the termites had eaten every stick of timber out of the attached rooms on the old homestead. They had tunnelled through the walls of the building and could be heard gnawing away inside the house timbers at night, reducing the beams and rafters to a painted paper-thin shell. Sid decided it was time to move out and make way for a better airstrip.

To avoid the termites, the new homestead, which was due for completion at the end of the wet season, was constructed on black soil country 300 yards from the old site. The sheds were moved and the mud walls knocked over and smashed up to provide filling for the gilgais on the runway of the upgraded airstrip. When this was finished, it represented a great step forward because it enabled a weekly mail plane and the Flying Doctor to land in all seasons.

Jack and Dulcie settled upon a comfortable six room dwelling with a flywire verandah all round. It was steel-framed with a cyprus pine floor which was elevated three feet above the ground to discourage termites. A carpenter was provided by Sidney Williams and Co, who supplied the house and the brothers did much of the labouring. Digging the many postholes for the stumps in the hard black soil without a posthole-digger was heavy work. When the stumps were concreted in place, the carpenter assembled and bolted the sections together prior to erection, much like a meccano set.

Between 1942, when Lucy returned to Queensland, and April 1948, when Jack brought his wife home, 'Eva Downs' had been a bachelor establishment. Olive and her fiancee, Ron Price, came up for a while to help Dulcie set up the new house. Colin was in the stockcamp and Alf was attending a muster at 'Anthony's Lagoon'. Bill, who was mechanically-minded and preferred to be the handyman, remained at the station building new sheds and horse yards. He was available to lend the two women a hand when they needed one. For some unaccountable reason Jack took offence when the women expressed their appreciation for Bill's assistance. The two brothers had such a major disagreement that Bill sold his interest in the property and returned to Queensland.

Sid was getting on in years and Bill's action prompted him to relinquish his share too. Alf suggested it should be transferred to Colin in recognition of his years of unpaid labour. Jack, who never agreed with anyone but himself, objected strongly but he was eventually persuaded. The three brothers then became equal partners. When increased cattle sales improved their fortunes, they took it in turns to remain at the station during the wet season, while the other two had a holiday. A skeleton staff was all that was required at that time of year because the rain replenished the surface water and the cattle were not dependent on the bores.

During this period preparation for the next year's cattle mustering was done. All the saddles and leather gear were overhauled, cleaned and greased. Yard repairs were carried out when it was dry enough and a good bit of time was spent making branding ropes and hobbles from sides of leather and greenhide to ensure there was a good supply on hand.

Sid, now semi-retired, divided his time between Mungallala and 'Eva'. He liked to keep on the move and be busy. When he was on the property, he filled the position of caretaker-cook and spent a lot of time in the garden growing vegetables. One Christmas Day two of the boys were lazing around on their beds reading when Sid said, "We'll have lunch a bit early. I have put a plum duff on for lunch; now I'm off to the vegetable garden, so I'll leave it to you fellows to see the duff doesn't boil dry and to make some custard to go with it." The menu for Christmas lunch was corned leg of goat with plum pudding boiled in a cloth. When the boys looked around on the stove for the duff, expecting to find it in the boiler their mother had used for the purpose, they could find no sign of it. There was a large beef bucket of water boiling on the stove from which protruded the shank of corned goat and saucepans containing vegetables sat on the hob. At first they thought that Sid had forgotten to put on the duff, but after a hunt around they spotted a piece of cloth in the beef bucket and found the missing pudding. The boys made the custard but they didn't hold out much hope for the duff. They thought that it would taste like goat. To their surprise it was excellent, having been effectively sealed by the flour inside the calico cloth.

That Christmas Day was considerably better than another Alf spent a couple of years later when he came upon a bore where a cow had died upside down in the water trough. In her dying moments she had wrecked the float, which in turn released all the water from the earth tank. The 1,700 head of cattle on the bore had to be shifted to another watering point on Christmas Day, so lunch was out of a saddle bag.

One of the interesting features on 'Eva Downs' was what was referred to as the lakes or flood-out area. After heavy monsoonal rain the flood-out spread across the southern part of the Barkly Tableland. It extended from Lake Woods near 'Newcastle Waters' in the north, almost 400 miles through a shallow depression, to Lake Nash in the south-east. In some places they were thirty to forty miles wide. Although a large expanse of water, the lakes were very shallow. Lake Sylvester on 'Brunette Downs' and Lake Woods were the biggest and slightly deeper, taking three drought years to dry up completely. On 'Brunette' a couple of higher ridges formed islands where cattle were sometimes trapped by the water. To prevent them starving, stockmen transported their saddles by boat to the island and led their horses. Once on the island they mustered the cattle and swam them back.

With the exception of a few deeper channels, a tall man could walk through the flood-out area when it was full. Along one part of its northern shore, one of the deeper parts ran onto a beach with a pebbly embankment resembling a sand dune. It was some six to eight feet high in places and at its base bleached mussel and snail shells could be found. On either side of the two mile beach the normal ash grey or black soil resumed.

The lake country was a bovine paradise because it was covered with bluebush, lignum, fine waterweeds, and a variety of other herbage which was naturally irrigated. When the wind blew for a few days the water was swept out half a mile or so in the opposite direction. As the wind changed so did the sheet of water. It was good country when the seasons were kind but when the monsoons failed it became very dry. Fortunately, the bluebush was hardy and survived to support the cattle.

When full, these swamps or lakes teamed with a huge variety of nesting waterfowl — brolgas, pelicans, ducks, jabiru, ibis of all species, plovers, magpie geese etc. Flocks of ibis often hovered above in a clouds which cast a giant shadow. Their rookeries were on top of dense clumps of flattened lignum bushes about two feet high. When laid, the eggs were safely suspended above the water and there were thousands of nests crowded together over the four acres of lignum bushes.

Normally, by the time mustering started, the water had receded and the chicks followed the water in. In the lake country dawn was always heralded by an orchestra of water birds. The raucous squawks of the brolgas, the quacking of ducks and the trumpeting of magpie geese. Once when Lake Woods dried up, the geese led their young by the hundreds into Elliott township. Magpie geese found on the poorer coastal country fattened well and were good eating but for some inexplicable reason those on the better Barkly country never seemed to fatten and weren't good to eat.

Wild duck did fatten well. One year in open duck-shooting season a keen shooter went to the lakes with Alf. They returned through the sticky mud with a bag of fifty ducks, mostly of the smaller teal variety. The birds weren't that big, but very fat and sweet. At the homestead the family had gone visiting and there were only two ringers in the men's quarters, relaxing and reading westerns. The two shooters asked the ringers for a hand to pluck and clean the ducks under a shady tree close to the quarters.

"You shot them, you pluck them," was the response.

"Yes," said Alf, "But I bet you won't be backward in coming forward to eat them."

"For sure we'll oblige you then, don't worry," they assured him.

Half-way through the plucking, a drover came along and after talking for a while he noticed the extra-long-barrelled gun used to shoot the ducks.

"Is it any good?" asked the drover.

"Of course it is," replied Alf's shooting mate. "You just get that much closer with it. Alf uses it, kills both ends at times."

"Here, you have a shot. Knock those two crows sitting together on the tree." It was about fifty yards away. The drover let fly and killed both crows. He went over and plucked the breast feathers off the birds to see where the shot hit and said, "Gee, they are fat." It was then that Alf had an inspiration. He decided to cook the two crows for the ringers.

The next night Dulcie cooked a feast of duck and in a separate dish, the two crows. She served the ducks onto the plates and took them to the table then called Alf to serve the two crows to the ringers. The two chaps lapped them up and backed up for a second helping. When they got back to the quarters, another ringer thought the joke too good to keep to himself and spilt the beans. One of the crow-eaters immediately put his finger down his throat but next day he saw the joke and laughed about it. He recalled the gun shot and the fact that Alf had served their dinner and when he found the crow feathers near the duck feathers under the tree, he was convinced.

He asked Alf, "Anyway, which was the crow — the first helping or the last?" When Alf answered the first, he said, "Good Lord. It was better than the last. You had better shoot more crows in future." The other bloke refused to believe he had eaten crow but when all the evidence proved otherwise, he asked for his cheque and left. In Elliott someone asked him why he left a good job and he replied sourly, "It's time to leave when they start feeding you crow, isn't it?"

Even though there was an abundance of wild fowl on the lakes, the Aboriginal people never ventured into them, referring to the area as 'divel divel' country. They hated mustering cattle there. Anyway, when the lakes were full, there was an abundance of bush tucker in the surrounding higher country, so it was unnecessary for them to hunt at the lakes. On little limestone outcrops the giant goanna of central Australia was common. It had a habit of standing up on its tail and hind legs when curious. They grew to six feet or more and a really big one stood two feet six inches high, when up on its hind legs.

At Tarrabool Lake one day when mustering stock, a young Aboriginal chap came up with an enormous grin on his face. He was very proud of a large fat goanna, probably weighing nearly forty-five pounds, he had slung across the pommel of his saddle. The reptile was held by the neck to prevent it biting as well as being well and truly hobbled. A toenail on each foot had the skin and the bone cut allowing the nail to be pulled out several inches while still attached to the sinew. The back legs were tied in a knot above its back and the front legs were tied in the same manner. This method was used to transport the goanna back to the station fresh for a corroboree. A similar thing was often done with wild ducks to keep them fresh until needed. Both legs and wings were broken to immobilise the bird.

It seemed that the sand goanna was much preferred to the tree goanna which was a carrion-eater. The Aborigines mainly hunted with dogs during the wet season walkabout time, when the reptiles were very fat. It wasn't uncommon to see several Aborigines with live goannas tied onto the back of their saddles during a day's muster. At times a goanna's head was placed in a shirt sleeve and the legs and tail tied to the crupper dee on the back of the saddle. Alf tried goanna a couple of times but never developed a taste for it.

The arrival of enormous mobs of brolgas circling over the station lagoons was a good indication that Tarrabool Lake down on 'Eva's' eastern border, a good twenty miles ride from the homestead, might be drying up. When this happened, there was a danger of cattle being stranded without water, so someone always went out to investigate. On one occasion Colin and Alf took a couple of water bottles with them and rode to the lake and found it dry. The lake was the watering point for about 900 cattle, about eighty percent were 'Anthony's Lagoon' stock and the rest belonged to 'Eva'. The men settled down beneath a nice shady coolibah tree and waited for the cattle to return to where the last water had been. They were then mustered and taken to the next nearest water at Tarrabool Waterhole.

It took a while to put them together and start them in the right direction through the grey crumbly ground. After a couple of miles the horses were nearly knocked up, when some old 'Anthony's Lagoon' cows started to lead out, knowing they were going to get a drink at Tarrabool Waterhole. Colin and Alf decided the best way to make progress was for one of them to walk behind the tail of the mob while the other rode and led the spare horse. A man on foot was able to make the young calves take more notice and walk along. The lead of the mob reached the waterhole before darkness fell and the others slowly followed. It was a relief to see the rising moon shining on the big sheet of shallow water. After the old breeders had their fill, they returned to their tardy, bellowing offspring. When they found the right calf, they gave it a drink of milk and went contentedly off to graze.

Once the men, who had been thirsty for hours, were satisfied that all the cattle were watered and the calves mothered up, they took a good long drink themselves.

The exhausted horses were unsaddled and their backs given a good wash down before being hobbled and let go to graze. Colin and Alf had to be satisfied with a dingo's dinner — a drink of water and a look around. It didn't matter much because they were full of water and too tired to feel hungry. More than anything they needed a good sleep. About three o'clock in the morning, Alf was wakened by a weird shaking sensation. For about four minutes he had a giddy feeling, as though he was about to throw a fit. Colin hadn't stirred, so Alf thought the experience was entirely his own and didn't mention it in the morning. When they arrived home he was relieved that what he feared was a fit was in fact an earthquake. Its centre was somewhere off Darwin and the tremor was felt as far south as Tennant Creek. After their twenty-four hour fast Dulcie fed them like fighting cocks and told them how the house had shaken so violently that all the china in the cupboards rattled.

In later years the border fence went through the flood-out country. For the first few years after the fence was built and the area was drying out it had to be watched closely. Once Alf drove there after a strong westerly wind had been blowing for nearly a week and was alarmed to find 3,000 head of cattle parading up and down the fence. They were able to see the sheet of water but were unable to get to it. He raced home, got two men and a plant of horses and in order to be on the job at first light, they rode until two o'clock in the morning. The wind was almost gale force and had changed to a south-easterly as first light approached. When they rode out, they found that plenty of water had been swept by the wind back through the fence line and the cattle were all watered and happily grazing. It was an incredible natural irrigation system which watered all the soft herbage and bluebush pasture. To prevent a similar emergency in the future, Alf and his men drove the cattle to a bore four miles away to show them where they could find water when next the flood-out receded.

Prior to the erection of the boundary fence and when there was a lot more water about, Alf joined the 'Anthony's Lagoon' stockcamp to help muster that same area of flood-out country. Many 'Eva Downs' cows and unbranded calves were found. Wanting to be sure he had all of the potential branders, Alf said, "Give me one of those kids and we'll go on right round this sheet of water to see what there is on the other side. We should do it in half a day."

As Alf and the twelve year old Aboriginal stockboy rode through the low-lying coolibah and lignum country, increasing cloud obscured the sun. They had gone a fair distance when the horse Alf rode had a heart attack, so he had to leave it, hang his saddle in a tree and start walking. The boy was told to stay on the other horse out in front, so he could see over the low timber and get a better sense of direction than the man on foot. To circle the area all they had to do was stay out of the boggy mud and keep in sight of the big sheet of water on their left hand side.

When Alf became tired and swapped positions with the boy he found that the water on the left had disappeared and was now on the right hand side. He was completely bamboozled and thought that they had somehow changed direction. The boy assured Alf that was not the case. Their situation was quite serious as they were rapidly becoming dehydrated in the intense heat. The previously boggy ground was pock-marked with the impressions of cattle hooves. When a providential thunderstorm fell in the mid-afternoon, they were able to suck up the water which collected in those hoof prints.

The horse they shared had been born at 'Anthony's Lagoon' and Alf felt sure that if given its head it would take them home. The boy was convinced that he could lead them back and when it was his turn to ride he wouldn't give the horse its head. Eventually Alf could see he was thoroughly bushed and took the reins away from him and let the horse do the navigating. The tired animal needed constant urging. At one stage they crossed their earlier tracks which proved that they had ridden in a circle as intended. They were sure slewed.

Alf's faith that the horse would take them home was confirmed when at sundown the clouds lifted and the sun blazed out briefly right behind them. About eleven o'clock in the evening the poor animal was so exhausted, it was unsaddled and hobbled to prevent it wandering off. The pair had no swags so they made a rough mattress by pressing down big lignum bushes which suspended them fifteen inches above the soggy ground. It was an uncomfortable night because there was a multitude of crawling, biting insects. The certain knowledge that spiders, scorpions, centipedes and death-adders lurked in the darkness didn't help.

Next morning the sky was clear and they proceeded towards the sunrise and came out of the flood-out country towards the horse's home at 'Anthony's Lagoon' No. 12 station bore. Camel Ned, an Aboriginal stockman-cum-boundary rider lived there with his wife, Topsy. As a youth, Ned worked with an Afghan carting supplies with a camel team, from Burketown to 'Alexandria Downs'. They had a rest and a good feed and started back to the stockcamp on fresh horses. Fortunately they met the search party from the camp on their way. Alf drafted the 'Eva' cattle from the mustered mob, before the 'Anthony's Lagoon' cattle were put onto a camp for open bronco branding of all cleanskin calves.

This was not an ideal method of branding but useful when no yards were available. A make-shift branding bail was made using a couple of trees. Preferably the centre one had a forked trunk about four or five inches apart. One trunk is cut off about four feet high, from which a couple of rails are slanted off slightly towards the ground about eight or nine feet out. A post is put in to secure the other end, thus making a barrier for a man on a broncho horse. His job was to rope a calf from the mob held together on camp by a team of riders. The rope between the bellowing, protesting calf and the broncho horse passed over the top rail of the panel and the calf was then dragged up to it and the rope secured in the slot between the double trunks of the tree. When released after their ordeal the smaller calves ran back to their mothers and the protection of the big mob. Weaned calves, of which there were many, behaved quite differently. When released, they went bush. It was usually best to just let them go and hope that they had forgotten the experience by the time they were mustered next.

Camel Ned, who was an excellent tracker, had back-tracked the horse Alf and the boy had ridden when they were lost and found the saddle in the tree and the animal dead beside it. The 'Anthony's Lagoon' manager questioned Johnnie, who was Ned's brother and born on 'Eva' fifty years before, about a lake further on than Tarrabool.

"Oh yes, I been there years ago as a young fellow with old 'Yabba' Harry a couple of times."

In the early 1920's 'Brunette Downs' also held the old 'Eva Downs' blocks and 'Yabba' Harry had been the caretaker/manager of the outstations. His name was Harry Thomas and he got his nickname from the Aborigines because of his constant chattering. He worked for 'Brunette' for twenty-three years before they relinquished the 'Eva' blocks and his services were terminated. Harry was not impressed, stating, "I never would have taken their lousy employment at all if I thought it wasn't going to be a permanent job!"

Alf was very puzzled about the lake waters changing from one side to the other, so much so that he decided to charter an aeroplane to look over it. He contacted Connellan Airways and when the plane came with the mail, the pilot, Col Johnson, flew him over the lake country. The mystery was quickly solved. When attempting to circle the lake by keeping the water on their left hand side they had passed between two sheets of water, the other a couple of miles or so to the south of the first one. Because of Alf's experience there it became known as Perishing Lake. Plenty of cattle were seen on it from the air and as the stock were on the boundary a combined 'Anthony's Lagoon', 'Rockhampton Downs' and 'Eva' stockcamp was organised for the muster.

Mustering Perishing Lake was extremely hard on horses, bogging round, sometimes up to their bellies in mud, all day. After floundering through the mud for twenty or thirty yards, they were usually too frightened to take a good drink and were thirsty again a couple of hours later. The only horse feed was a soft mossy grass which cattle did well on, but it tended to make horses thirsty.

The flight also revealed another lake on 'Eva' with a few cattle on it, so three of the brothers took a packhorse camp down to muster them. They were mainly their own cows plus a good number of unbranded cleanskin bulls and heifers. Some of these cattle, though quiet enough, had never seen a rider. They kept breaking from the mob and a couple had to be tipped over and and leg strapped while the remainder of the mob was put around them. The cattle were then driven around a bit to educate the new ones to stay with the mob. With the mustering completed and darkness not far off, they decided to night-watch the herd, taking a third of the night each. The cattle camp was carefully chosen without undergrowth and a number of dead coolibahs surrounding it. These were set on fire to keep the cattle on camp. The beacons of light seemed to mesmerise the cattle but falling limbs occasionally gave the mob a start and the riders had to take care not to be struck by them. Next day the cattle were walked home for branding.

Mustering the flood-out country provided many dangers and surprises. In the mid-fifties Alf and his team went out to collect cattle from a lake. There was a cattle pad leading across a small channel into an area that was surrounded by water. Alf left his team on the other side of the channel while he followed the pad to check if there were any cattle on the isolated strip of land. He located a small mob on very boggy ground and by the time he had rounded them up his horse was well and truly knocked up. Once the cattle were walking well, he let the horse go and walked behind them.

It was then that he noticed a buffalo in the middle of the cattle. Lone buffaloes out of their territory could be very dangerous, especially to a man on foot. Usually they had been hunted out of their own herd by other bulls and likely to have been wounded in a fight or by buffalo hunters. This one had an impressive set of horns and its head was tilted back sniffing the air. Buffaloes have very poor eyesight and rely on their acute sense of smell to locate danger. It was obviously confused by the movement of the cattle and trying to locate the cause.

Realising that he was on foot and in imminent danger, Alf tried to keep down wind of the animal and concealed himself behind the sparse timber. Knowing he was very vunerable on foot without adequate cover he proceeded cautiously. When they were close to the channel he could see the mounted riders on the other side and called to them for help. Even though they were mounted, they were very wary of the buffalo and were reluctant to come to his assistance. As it turned out, when the buffalo caught sight of the riders, it took off into the bush and lived to fight another day.

The weekly mail plane on the airstrip in front of the homestead.

Bronco branding.

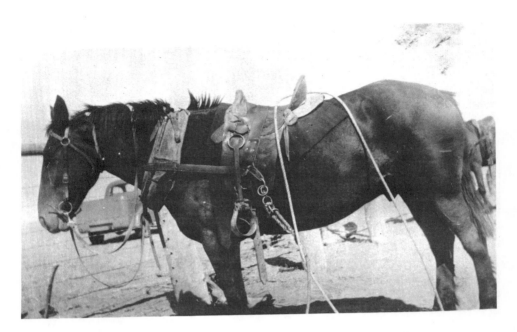

Bronco horse used for pulling the calf up the the bronco panel.

Bruce Simpson and the ex-army Blitz truck.

13.

Sighting the Posts and the Pickets

When pleuropneumonia started to spread to the 'Eva' herd from the cattle depot next door, the boys tried to limit their stock losses by erecting a fence on their western boundary. Barbed wire for fencing was hard to obtain during the war so the Chambers were very pleased when Western Grazing Company offered them a shipment of barbed wire in exchange for erecting the forty mile fence, using steel posts and timber strainers. They decided to do twenty miles that year and twenty the next. Once they had started on this section of the boundary fencing, it was decided to keep pressing on until the total boundary of 132 miles was completed. Money, materials and time were the limiting factors. Sometimes neighbours employed a contractor to do their half share while others got the Chambers to complete a whole line and paid half the costs. It was many years before the entire job was finished.

It became essential to improve the cattle yards. A good long crush was needed in order to vaccinate the herd against pleuropneumonia. Timber for yards was very scarce, so bloodwood posts were cut on 'Shandon Downs' and the lancewood rails on 'Mungabroom', some distance away to the north.

Following some storms which filled small waterholes in the area, the boys loaded crosscut saws and sharp axes, which were difficult to cart on packhorses, into the old twin seater buggy pulled by a couple of strong chain horses. The horses and buggy made a track which was later followed by a team of horses pulling Dave Cahill's tabletop wagon loaded with the cut posts. This was preferable to the truck because sharp stakes couldn't pierce the tyres.

It was extremely hot, still weather when they attacked the post cutting with crosscut saws in the low turpentine scrub. Work was done in the early morning and late afternoon to avoid the midday heat. On the last evening a strong north-easterly wind blew up which they suspected might result in rain, so they lowered the fly hoping to run off the water. When the storm hit, the wind was so fierce that rain simply blew in one end and out the other and they were grateful for the protection offered by their birkmyre swag covers. The stout little bloodwood tree that supported the fly withstood the gale-force winds during the long night of heavy but intermittent rain. It didn't ease up about nine o'clock in the morning.

Everything was soaking wet, but they managed to light a fire and have a light breakfast before harnessing the horses and starting on the twenty-three mile trip back to the homestead. On the way they noticed the bauhinia, coolibah and supplejack trees uprooted by the storm and lying on the ground. Back at the station they heard on the wireless that the big storm was in fact a cyclone. Nine and a half inches of rain had fallen but fortunately the cyclone had not done much damage to buildings apart from some erosion where the rain had pelted in on one of the mud brick walls of the old house. Other properties in the cyclone's path suffered structural damage to buildings and windmills.

Preparations for the job of carting the posts took a day or two. The team horses were mustered from a spell-horse paddock and the following day were driven to Dave Cahill's place where they were hobbled out. The next morning the sixteen horses were harnessed to the empty wagon and driven to where the posts were to be collected. Once again the horses were hobbled for the night before they started snigging and loading at the main patch. The worst part of carting the posts was having to load them up two sloping rails onto the seven foot high table top wagon. This was done with a wire rope attached to the wagon rails at one end and looped over the top of each post. A horse then pulled the other end of the rope from the other side of the wagon. It was such a slow job that they made sure the logs didn't fall off once loaded.

A full load was collected and they started back to 'Eva' the next day. The next load was harder to collect as the timber was much more scattered and the team had to stand still at the various locations while the posts were loaded.

Dave offered to loan them his team horses, but the boys knew they had bolted a few times and preferred to use their own. Lucky they did, because shortly afterwards Dave attempted to use his team to cart posts onto his boundary fence line and the horses bolted and the wagon came to a halt when it collided with a stout tree. The horses then wrapped themselves round the whole wagon, shearing off the shafts. The massive old wagon remained up on that spinifex ridge and was soon riddled with white ants. In about five years all that was left were the eight inch broad steel wheel rims, cast iron axles and a great heap of bolts and fittings that once held it all together.

While Jack's house was being built, Alf was out on the run with Dave Cahill and several Aboriginal stockmen, shifting cattle from rapidly drying waters. About mid afternoon one mob of about 4,500 head was taken off an almost dry lake and started over the cracked downs country for Surveyor's Hole, some twelve miles away. With no road to follow and a lot of young calves to push along after their mothers, progress was slow for the first half of the journey. Soon after midnight a cool breeze sprang up and a halt was called, so the men could have a feed while the trailing cows and calves had a spell.

During the meal break Dave said, "I wonder if those nephews of mine arrived at 'Eva' yet? What a pity they didn't arrive yesterday. This would have been a great breaking in for them with the heat we have had today." He was expecting his three nephews to arrive from County Cork in Ireland. He had sent them prepaid air tickets to Darwin and given them directions to travel on Tuits passenger bus to Elliott. Once there, they had to hitch a ride out to 'Eva' on a Works and Housing truck. Dave had to collect a load of barbed wire and intended to pick up his nephews at the same time with his team and wagon.

The moon came out and a good head-wind kept the calves cool as they pushed the cattle onto Surveyor's Hole. After sleeping for an hour or so, Dave headed for home to pick up his team horses and wagon and Alf returned to the homestead and arrived shortly after the three nephews. The poor fellows were travel-weary and feeling the heat. They had brought themselves a water bag from which they each took frequent swigs. Even the short walk from the old house to the one under construction was interrupted half-way for a drink.

They had never met their supposedly rich uncle and they began to interrogate Alf about him. "What kind of car do he drive?"

When told Uncle Dave had never owned nor driven a car in his life, one of them said, "For sure, this is a big disappointment. We thought the rich Uncle with his big expanse of land would drive up to meet us in his limousine, armed with a case of champagne."

Then they asked, "Where do he go to chapel then and how far is the nearest Holy Roman House of God?"

They weren't impressed when Alf told them that the closest church was in Tennant Creek, 190 miles away and that Dave never at any time went to church. One chap remarked, "For sure, the man is a heathen. We shall have to boycott him."

Next day Bill had to take the truck out past where Dave was camped pumping water with an old steam engine, so he took the nephews along. After Bill had introduced them, Dave asked, "Where are your swags and quart pots? You're no good in this country without those." Then calling to his Aboriginal stockman, "Jim Ross, make these fellows a quart pot each out of a fruit tin, so they can have a drop of tea." When the Irish lads went off round the other side of the steam engine to compare notes on their uncle, Dave remarked conspiratorially to Bill, "I think my sister has sent me out an inferior type of Irishmen."

He set them to work straight away on the eight miles of his southern boundary fence line, which was overdue for completion. Several days later, on a very hot day, a bush fire came through the spinifex country along this fence. A three ton pile of black barbed wire nicely stacked upon hardwood rails caught fire. In the extreme heat, the wooden spools inside the twenty-eight pound coils caught fire and melted the wire into a pool of lava. The stack resembled a miniature volcano, with molten metal running over three to four feet around the surrounding area.

When Dave next turned up at 'Eva' to collect another load of barbed wire, he was asked what he thought of his nephews. "One won't work at all. He's only fit to make a policeman. One won't talk at all, and the another is all talk. They are just not interested in taking over the place at all, so I think I will put it on the market as I am getting too old to carry on. I offered it to them for a small rental, just enough for me to live on, and one fellow said, "And just how old do you have to be to get the old aged pension in this country?"

After a month the youngest chap had gone off to Brisbane and the other two remained to complete the fence line. One day when Alf chanced to meet them, one of the nephews said, "All we want to do is go home. For sure we may be lucky enough to get a call home to fight the English one day." Not long after that Dave paid his fare to Ireland and put the place on the market. It was soon sold to the Scottish Australian Company who owned 'Anthony's Lagoon'. One nephew remained caretaking on 'Shandon Downs' until all the cattle were mustered for delivery, and for a while on 'Anthony's Lagoon'. After nearly thirty years in the Territory, Dave went off for a long overdue holiday, got married and lived to the ripe old age of eighty-three years.

II   Putting up the Boundary Fences

Out on the runs towards sundown —
Out where the lone stations are,
There are many bridle hands gripping
The shovel and wielding the bar.
The men who once lived in the saddle,
Have put leggings and goosenecks away,
The drovers who once swung the road mobs,
Are out swinging axes today.

Bruce Forbes Simpson

Towards the end of the 1952 drought work such as bore drilling and fencing was going ahead. No cattle were being moved, so there were many drovers out of work and seeking alternative employment until the seasons improved. The brothers and their cousin Doug were joined by drover, Bruce Simpson, who came to them seeking agistment for his plant of horses. Bruce took over Doug's job tailing the horses, freeing him to help Alf erect windmills.

The Leigh Brothers of 'Brunchilly' on 'Eva's southern border had employed two out of work drovers, Bill Crowson and Bill Tapp, to erect their half of the boundary fence, so it was imperative that the 'Eva' fencing team got on with their half. Crowson and Tapp were soon to hear the good news that they had successfully balloted for 'Montejinne' and 'Killarny', once outstations of Victoria River Downs. More small landholders to swell the growing ranks.

As the fence was in the flood-out area from Attack Creek, it was also essential that the job be completed before the onset of the wet season. First a road was fire-ploughed from the new D bore in the south-west of the property south along Attack Creek for about twelve miles. The western boundary fence which was completed the previous year was only a few miles from the new road.

With Bruce Simpson and a good team of men the fourteen miles of fencing were completed before the thunder storms and Jack and Colin went on holidays. Bruce then stayed on to help the 'Brunchilly' contractors. Alf planned to go to Elliott for the New Year Races and return with a new employee, Ray Lewis. The day before the mail plane arrived, he checked all the watering points and was confident all would be well in his absence. The plane took him to Tennant Creek where he visited the doctor to have a painful whitlow on his thumb lanced before going on to the races.

The night before Alf and Ray Lewis were to return to 'Eva' by truck, a cyclone came in over Borroloola. There were reports of heavy rain on the stations all around 'Eva'. Sixteen inches at 'Anthony's Lagoon', seventeen at 'Cresswell Downs, thirteen at 'Brunette Downs', sixteen at 'Rockhampton Downs', and so on. The cyclone came back over 'Brunchilly', 'Banka Banka', 'Helen Springs' and Elliott, which all received similar heavy falls.

Motor transport was now out of the question, so Alf borrowed a horse and saddle and set out on the 110 miles through the mud. Because of the boggy conditions he could only travel about thirty miles in a day. As he got closer to home, he noticed there had been much less rain and the steep-sided creek, which he anticipated having to swim, was only four feet deep. The horse was able to walk across but because the saddle had no breast plate and the animal was herron-gutted, when it scrambled up the far bank the saddle slipped over its rump and Alf was dumped unceremoniously at the water's edge. At sundown when he finally arrived home he was absolutely amazed to see dust blowing on the airstrip and the rain in the gauge measured only 110 points. It appeared that the storms had fallen all around 'Eva'.

Ray Lewis wasn't able to come out by truck and arrived three days later with his plant of horses. There was no grass whatsoever in the horse paddocks following the drought, so the 'Eva' horses had all been allowed the run of the property to survive. Now that there was some grass beginning to grow, Alf decided to muster them so the young ones could be branded, the colts castrated and the working horses put into spell paddocks ready for the coming season's work.

Although the cyclone had gone all round, the run off from the heavy rain in the north, east and south started to drain into the flood-out country ensuring a good season for stock feed. The drought was broken. In exceptional wet seasons pilots reported a great sheet of water thirty-five miles long and twenty miles across. Two-thirds of this was on 'Eva Downs', the remainder on 'Anthony's Lagoon' and 'Rockhampton Downs'.

More fencing was completed each year and by 1953, the south-east corner remained the only unfenced boundary. This was because it was the most difficult, as it passed through twenty-three miles of dry-ash, grey flood-out soil. During the heavy wet seasons the area was sometimes submerged beneath five feet of water. The six and a half miles along the 'Eva'-'Rockhampton Downs' boundary travelling east-west was tackled first. The other twelve and a half miles which ran north-south between 'Eva' and 'Anthony's Lagoon' was a shared effort.

The three ton ex-army Blitz truck used for the 'Rockhampton Downs' boundary fencing broke through the loose soil, at one stage sinking up to the mudguards. This dry bog was unbelievably bad and the worst they had ever encountered. The tyres had cut down to more solid ground and supported the weight of the truck. The three men spent half a day lying on their sides to clear the loose soil away from the chassis, then cutting and carting green coolibah leaves and small branches to place in front of all the wheels. It was a great relief to get the job done.

In 1958 'Eva Downs' became the first grazing property in the Northern Territory to completely fence its boundary. The battlers had beaten the big boys again. The Chambers were relieved to keep most of the cattle on the run and save a lot of extra work chasing strays. On occasions when stock sometimes broke through fences they attended neighbouring musters.

As a precaution against further outbreaks of disease caused by infected cattle being dropped among the herd, it was decided to fence the one mile wide stockroute that ran through 'Eva'. It also reduced the likelihood of their cattle, mistakenly or otherwise, being included in passing drover's mobs. The Lands Department willingly sent out a surveyor to peg the proposed fence line. As the fence posts were cut, they were carted and dropped on the spot ready to be stood up. The fence construction was of timber posts a chain apart interspersed with steel droppers and strung with two barb and one plain wire.

The materials were trucked out from Mt. Isa. Digging postholes was a thing of the past because the station now owned a a Massey Ferguson 35 tractor complete with posthole digger and a post-borer which attached to the three point linkage. Now all that was required was a team of men to erect the fence.

It was mid-October when Alf went looking for men. The season's droving and mustering was about done, so he looked for ringers willing to get off a horse and pick up a shovel and crow bar. Most of them thought it beneath their dignity and he had no takers in Camooweal, so he went on to Mt. Isa. Here he came across three young chaps strapped for cash, two of whom had run foul of the law in Camooweal. They were willing to take on anything. One chap was a ringer and refused to pick up a crow bar but was willing to pull and tie wire and cook. He had never cooked before, but did a fair job on the open fire and kept the camp clean and tidy, often reminding the other boys of their responsibilities in this regard.

The other two chaps were right for the job too. A tall, strapping bloke called Slim, kept the team in good spirits with his tireless energy and jovial spirits. He claimed to be the best educated member of the trio, having served a term in Westbrook Youth Detention Centre. Although he highly recommended the discipline in that institution he couldn't say the same for the academic side of the curriculum. The Camooweal police constable had asked Slim to hand in his unregistered, long barrel .38 calibre revolver, but being a juvenile deliquent he threw it into the Georgina River instead.

The other youth's name was Kevin and he had an affair with a carefree, under-age lass — an offence entailing a gaol term at that time — who found herself pregnant and named him as the father. If he didn't marry the girl, her mother threatened to turn him over to the police. Kevin left town under a cloud and in a hurry. He had a lot of trouble keeping up with Slim at first, especially when the bitumen from the steel posts burnt his face and hands badly, causing blisters. Slim kept urging him on saying, "Come on, you sexy little bugger, Kevin!" He was a good worker and stayed on at 'Eva' until after the birth of the child, when another chap accepted responsibility and married the girl.

The job progressed well and in three weeks twenty-one miles was completed and they were near No. 3 bore. The cook came across a tremendous mob of flock pigeons that landed seeking water from the overflow. They were so thick he couldn't resist having a few shots at them. He bought home thirty-four to pluck and dress and the camp had pigeon pie, pigeon stew and curried pigeon for the next day or two. The birds were fat and beautiful eating, a pleasant change from the usual diet of salt beef.

When going past No.3 stockroute bore, the cook filled up the water drum, not realising that the water was considered unfit for human consumption. It caused both stock and people considerable flatulence which resulted in rude noises, vulgar comments and red faces. The boys wrongly blamed the pigeon diet for their blustery condition and one lad said, "If that is not fowl, I'm no judge of poultry."

There was a big disposal sale of surplus Government machinery held in Darwin, while Alf was still on the fencing job. Jack and Colin relieved him, so he could attend in order to buy a mechanical ripper to use in conjunction with the D4 'dozer to replace the horse-drawn road-plough that was still in use.

The northern section of the stockroute was fenced prior to the wet season, making a 250 square mile paddock to the north of the run. The area was watered by two new bores, two dams and Surveyor's Hole and some minor water holes. It so happened that the Barkly country adjacent to the Queensland border had missed out on reasonable rain and the Peel River Land and Mineral Company were seeking agistment for 'Avon Downs' breeding cows. Alf contacted them and said that there was a paddock available on 'Eva' that would take 4,000 head.

14

Watering the Stock

During the early fifties the Northern Territory Administration had a change of heart and started encouraging smaller settlers by balloting parcels of land. To the north west of 'Eva', the Beebe family took up 'Ucharonidge' and the Muller brothers, 'Mungabroom". The Government also put forward a scheme to assist incoming tenants by extending low-interest, long-term loans to put down two bores.

Several new bores were sunk on 'Eva' with the No. 2 Southern Cross boring plant and equipped with windmills, troughing and earth-tanks. A water storage dam called the Six Mile was also constructed. These earthmoving jobs were still being done with horse teams. The place selected for the Six Mile dam was the only good natural site on the property. It was where the headwaters of a small creek flowed between two iron stone hills which were about fifteen or twenty feet high. By closing the 130 yard gap between these two hills a lake about eight feet at the deepest point, and covering an area of twenty to thirty acres, was formed, before it overflowed round one of the hills. When completed, this impressive water storage was fifteen feet deep.

Initially, the problem was finding enough water for the horses near the work site. A timely storm solved the problem by filling the gilgais around the edge of the ironstone ridges. Half the embankment was built before the water gave out. The following year there was seven feet of water in the excavation and they were able to complete the wall at their leisure. It was a beautiful sight after the next wet season and took less work to build than the house dam, which was on a bigger creek and had no natural overflow.

During the 1952 drought the Barkly missed out on the monsoonal rains and a lot of places were running short of grass and the cattle were threatened with starvation. As a form of drought assistance the Northern Territory Administration offered to finance property owners to sink bores to limit livestock losses.

The cattle numbers on 'Eva' were increasing rapidly and as there was still a lot of undeveloped, unwatered country on the property, the brothers approached the

Government to finance four new bores. Following an inspection and site appraisal by the land officer, Gordon Buchanan, a loan was approved. He praised the Chambers for taking the initiative and sinking bores to maximise the potential of their unwatered country. In comparison, the management of 'Brunette Downs', which had unwatered but well grassed country on to the north of the property, chose not to sink bores to save their stock. The starving cattle were not shifted and it was rumoured that 30,000 head perished. At some bores, hundreds of dead cattle were dragged away from the water troughs into heaps.

Towards the end of the drought years two new bores were completed. They were named B and C to avoid confusion with the Government stockroute bores No's 2 and 3 which were in close proximity. Jack and Colin were the drillers on C bore, using the old Southern Cross boring plant that had come up from Queensland in 1937.

The motor had done a lot of work, greater than its capacity, and was using oil and blowing smoke. One brother said to the other, "She's knocking a bit."

"Rev her up, she'll be right."

With that the crankcase-housing disintegrated.

Fortunately a twenty-four foot Comet windmill had been installed on B bore so they were able to complete the job using the new Southern Cross motor from there as a substitute. As it was the dry season, the south-easterlies provided sufficient wind to pump water for the cattle.

Water was pumped into a temporary trough to water the chain horses used to build the earth-tank. Quite early in the piece, a lot of fine sand was pumped up the 190 feet of five inch pump column, which collected six inches deep in the trough and glittered with poor man's gold. Eventually the sand cut out the pump buckets and when the bore casing was pulled up it was found that sand was packed into the lower ten feet. It took a lot of freeing, but once done, little sand came up and the bore was soon operational. The brothers, including Bill who gave them a month of his time, and their cousin Doug Chambers, were all working on various jobs when they were joined by Bruce Simpson.

One morning Alf spotted a lame heifer at the trough. She had been mauled by dingoes and when she turned to walk off he could see that she was on three legs because the ham string of the other was broken. The only answer was to shoot her. The dingoes were bad during that drought and Alf wondered how many more animals had perished in the bush because of such attacks.

The next bore to be put down was D and it was necessary that this be done before the monsoons. D Bore was some sixteen miles from B Bore. The site was down the south-western section of the run near the flood-out area of a branch of Attack Creek. In the wet it flowed into a vast area of bluebush-covered, swampy country. The soil in that area was a dry ashy-grey or black which carried good Mitchell grass and bluebush pasture. A horse team pulled a fire plough to the bore site to make a road, then the horses were free to roam and take advantage of the good pasture.

While the others completed the troughing and fencing, Bruce Simpson helped Bill with the drilling of the bore. This was a heavy job for Bruce, who was only about eight and a half stone, slightly damp. When it came time to sharpen the 180 pound drill bit, it was put into a blacksmith's type forge to heat. Once it was glowing red, Bill attacked it with a sledge hammer until he was quite out of breath. Handing the hammer over, he said, "Here, Bruce, have a go!"

Bruce replied, "Hey listen, the name is Simpson, not Sampson!" None the less Bruce did take a turn for a while.

Because the bore was in low-lying country, abundant water was found quickly at 200 feet and the hole was easy to sink. This enabled Bill to assist building the earth-tank with the horse team. That was the last tank built using horse teams before a crawler tractor replaced them. The brothers realised it was high time to purchase a bulldozer. In 1956 they sent off two mobs of cattle which paid for a D4 Caterpillar dozer. As the two old trucks were pretty well worn out they also bought a six ton Chevrolet truck to transport the dozer up from Brisbane. Colin took delivery of the new machines and brought them back to 'Eva'. In the latter part of 1957 Colin, with the help of cousin Bob Chambers, completed the fifth bore and struck plenty of good water.

The horse teams served the Chambers well right up until 1956 when mechanization finally made them redundant. The natural increase in Sid's team horses wasn't very great because they were too big and heavy. As Jack and Alf did most of the livestock work, they made sure their saddle-horse breeding-stock were kept well segregated. 'Wave Hill' Freddie correctly described the Clydesdale cross stock horses as "Proper tumble down buggers." The brothers were not sorry when Sid's old stallions died of old age because they preferred to put a thoroughbred stallion over the heavy chain mares to get a more active bronco and pack horse.

In later years Harry Gorey, a veteran well-borer, was hired to sink more bores. Harry's reputation was so good that the brothers were confident enough to build earth-tanks and roads with the D4 bulldozer before he started drilling. The dozer worked day and night and was a great asset. It enabled many roads to be opened up to check watering points and earth tanks, that once took eight to ten weeks to build using horse teams, were completed in about five days.

Harry was a very interesting man and told many stories of his early days drilling. He was just on eighty years of age, strong and able to work hard all day. Every night before tea he sculled one large straight rum which he followed with a drink of water. He said that once when he was in hospital his wife smuggled in a coffee bottle of rum so that he could have a nip after lights out to make him sleep. When all was dark, he reached into his locker to retrieve the coffee bottle and poured an extra large nip into his glass and tossed it back as usual. It took his breath away and he collapsed onto the bed and the nurses had a hell of a job to wake him next morning. With daylight came the discovery that in the dark he had mistakenly poured himself a good slug of methylated spirits, which was kept in the locker in a similar container and used for back rubs.

Colin sunk two more bores a year later, which brought the total to eleven, not including the two Government stockroute bores, which could be rented in dry times. With adequate watering points scattered over the property, the "Eva' herd was able to make maximum use of the feed in the once waterless country.

15

On the Road with Eva Downs Cattle

To increase herd numbers at the end of the war the Chambers bought small men's turnoffs of cattle, at the right price. There was a very scattered bunch of 'Tandyigee' stragglers left behind among 'Beetaloo', 'Newcastle Waters' and 'Helen Springs' herds for which they offered a lump sum for whatever they could find. This resulted in quite a bit of work, attending musters on all three of these properties. Jack attended the 'Helen Springs' muster, Bill did a deal with Watty Bathern of 'Beetaloo' to collect what was there, which saved him having to cease drilling, and Alf attended the 'Newcastle Waters' muster.

Alf planned to do the 120 mile trip in four days, taking six horses and a packhorse. On the second day he came upon a drover, Jack Tweede, who had a mob of 400 shorthorn herd bulls travelling to 'Wave Hill'. He had gone past 'Eva Downs' three weeks previously, but had been requested to spell in a quarantine paddock at No. 6 bore to await a mob of old herd bulls from 'Helen Springs' to join in. The 'Helen Springs' bulls were quiet but cranky, and resented being held in a mob and night-watched and tried to wander off camp. Jack, seizing the opportunity of having an extra man to share the night watch, invited Alf to camp with him.

Jack was an old Kimberley drover who usually took bullocks into Wyndham Meat Works. He was a very tall, part-Aboriginal man, a rough rider of some repute and as deaf as a post. Trixie, his wife, was an Aborigine from Western Australia. The Wyndham Meat Works was closed due to the war so Jack had taken a mob from the Kimberleys into Queensland the previous year. An interesting feature of his droving camp were the nine pack donkeys which carried all the swags and camp gear. It was amazing the amount of weight that the small animals could carry. Their main failing was that they liked to set their own pace which was much slower than horses, so they were driven along by Trixie separate from the plant

Renner Springs Race Meeting.
Mounted left, Owen Lewis on Tor Spa.
Centre, John Auriac.
Right, Jack Chambers lodging a protest.

Shirley Begley, the nursing sister who became Alf's wife.

The Chambers Family.
The boys standing - Jack, Bill, Colin, Harry, Alf.
Seated Olive, Sid, Lucy, Daisy.

horses. Another donkey characteristic, if they weren't being driven, was to lie down on their bellies to take the weight off their backs. Jack said the 'donks' were smart little animals.

When he was taking the mob to Queensland the previous year, he was riding along in the lead of his bullocks, when he came upon Sid, chasing bush cattle out of the way of the travelling mob. One of Jack's stockmen gave an amusing account of what happened, when the two deaf men met.

"How far to the next water?" asked Jack.

"Speak up, I am a bit deaf," said Sid with his hand to his ear.

Jack put his hand to his ear saying, "I am a bit hard of hearing, what did you say?" This exchange went back and forth several times until Sid thought Jack was mocking him and he started to get wild. At this juncture Jack's man rode up beside Sid and shouted, "He is as deaf as a post. You have to yell at him." They both had a good laugh and proceeded to have a lengthy, shouted discussion.

Night-watching the bulls was quite an experience for Alf. The watches were split into three shifts. The horse tailer and Alf took the first three and a half hours. Trixie had two pet dogs plus a billy goat they were taking out to Halls Creek as a sire and change of blood for their goat herd. The goat had become quite attached to the two dogs that were the usual Heinz fifty-seven variety. Nevertheless they did bark at straying bulls. The 'poodles' barked and took an occasional snap at a bull's nose and the half-grown bleating goat followed them. Alf was amused because in his past experience strange noises were to be avoided when night-watching bullocks. Despite the noisy night-watch there was still a full count in the morning when he left to join the stockcamp at 'Newcastle Waters'.

The head stockman Fred Wilson, or 'Tragedy' as he was nicknamed, was a lightweight jockey-type and newly arrived on the job. He was glad to have Alf along, as he would have been the only white man in the camp of a dozen Aboriginal stockmen. He ran the station horses through the yard allocating each man his string of four horses. When one very nice chestnut horse came through, the stockmen all said, "He white man's horse", meaning the head stockman usually rode him. Fred was a bit wary and said to Alf, "Would you care to take a twist out of him first?" Alf agreed and found himself having the ride of his life, but he didn't come unstuck. Later they were told that the horse had been previously ridden by legendary horseman, Georgie Manphong. Manphong was a local lad descended from a Chinese cook and an Aboriginal mother. He could ride nearly anything.

In three weeks going down Newcastle Creek and out around Lake Woods they branded over 5,000 calves. The Wilsons were so grateful for Alf's assistance that instead of his having to call on one of his brothers to help him home with the seventy head of 'Tandyidgee'-branded cattle, they said, "Don't worry, we will lend you old Dick and his young son to see you home."

The Chambers soon realised what a threat the newly formed cattle depot next door at 'Helen Springs' posed to their herd. With more and more western cattle arriving, the prevalence of the dreaded pleuropneumonia increased and there were alarming losses experienced in the 'Eva' herd. Sid and the boys had to decide just what to do first. Inoculate the cattle to give them immunity or erect fencing to stop infected cattle coming through their western boundary.

Western Grazing Company offered them a shipment of barbed wire in exchange for erecting a forty mile fence on the western boundary. Despite the fencing and finding and shooting the carriers, the disease became more widespread in the herd making inoculation necessary. In order to do this, they extended a central set of cattle yards by building a long rail cattle crush and the immunisation was done using the old method.

The spread of pleuropneumonia was rife throughout the Top End during the late forties. Because some Vestey's drovers carelessly dropped off infected cattle on the stockroute rather than shooting them, it became known as Vestey's disease. The Government stock inspectors quarantined travelling mobs for lengthy periods to prevent further spread, which proved a good money spinner for some contract drovers. They were paid droving rates without having to shift camp which encouraged them to leave it up to the 'stocky' to find sick animals rather than detect them earlier themselves.

Initially the inspectors directed that some mobs be inoculated at the next convenient set of yards, but eventually it became a requirement that all mobs travelling the stockroute be inoculated by a Government stock inspector. This very smartly put an end to pleuropneumonia outbreaks in mobs travelling towards Queensland. The disease was so prevalent that failure by the stock owners to attend to this duty was plain carelessness or false economy.

Pleuropneumonia was not that noticeable in scattered small groups, but once cattle were crowded together in droving mobs, or a few thousand head came onto one watering point, outbreaks occurred. The disease spread rapidly during big musters when beasts were closely confined in the heat. After the 'Eva' herd was immunised, it showed a resultant increase in numbers which indicated just what a toll the unnoticed deaths had taken. Once pleuropneumonia was under control, a period of growth followed. Natural increase improved dramatically and cheaper lines of cattle were purchased. During the early fifties 800 head were bought from 'Montejinne' and 950 head from Roper Valley.

Air transport was improving and shorthorn stud breeders in southern New South Wales and Victoria, together with the Northern Territory Animal Husbandry Department director, Lionel Rose, decided to put on a stud bull sale at the 1950 'Brunette Downs' Races. The reasons were to promote the studs and encourage herd improvement in the Territory, where the shorthorn bloodlines were sadly lacking quality.

At that time Qantas Airways landed regularly at 'Brunette Downs' on their Sydney to Singapore run. As a promotional exercise, they offered to fly twenty show bulls up for the sale and the Federal Government also subsidised freight costs. The Chambers bought three of the stall-fed, fat, well groomed bulls. They were immunised against tick fever but it took time for them to acclimatise to the harsh northern conditions. The best bull died very quickly without leaving any progeny. The other two were so affected by the heat, buffalo fly and ticks in the first year that they didn't leave any calves behind either. Another two stud bulls were bought at an Alice Springs sale which bred prolifically, soon noticeably improving the quality of the herd.

W. B. Cameron was purchasing record numbers of cattle for fattening in southern Queensland and the Chambers brothers sold him 130 straggler bullocks. Doug Chambers and Alf took the mob to 'Brunette Downs', where they were to go into a droving mob. As they were unable to do long stages from yard to yard, Alf decided to do a little dog stiffening in his spare time.

At their first night's camp at No. 1 Bore, Jack delivered cooked tucker supplies plus a jute bag in which was a small leather pouch containing a bottle of strychnine. Next morning after washing up the cooking utensils, Alf packed everything away into packbags ready for Doug to load onto the packhorse and covered the camp fire to guard against a grass fire outbreak. Before riding off with the bullocks, he attached the small pouch of poison to the back of his saddle. He noticed that the lid on the bottle was loose and some of the contents had leaked into the new jute bag. Alf took the bag well out into long grass and discarded it, never suspecting Doug would come across it later.

On the return trip after delivering the cattle they found the country side ablaze and the fire threatened the horse paddocks. The two men successfully fought the fire and about 3 am returned to A Bore to camp. Doug suggested a cup of cocoa. The cocoa packet had broken open, so Doug had put it into a jute bag. The loose powder was scooped from the bottom of the bag into the pannikins and hot water added. Alf took the first mouthful and noticed the bitter taste and smartly spat it out. He then discovered that Doug, when helping to pack up the camp, had unwittingly retrieved the strychnine contaminated bag and put it to good use. The fact that Alf could have been responsible for giving them a lethal dose of strychnine was a sobering thought.

In the mid-fifties 'Eva' started to send off one good droving-sized mob of steers each year in charge of a drover. The animals were for sale and listed with the agents. Prospective buyers came and inspected them and the cattle were delivered to the buyers' destination. Mobs went all over western Queensland. One year two mobs were sent off. The second mob were of mixed sex, speyed cows and some staggy bullocks which before being taken to slaughter were agisted for fattening on the Hamilton River country. The agent had recommended the well fenced channel country for fattening cattle.

In the Hamilton River area a number of 250 square mile blocks were balloted and the successful drawers were small men, shearers, drovers, station hands etc., who were not overburdened with ready cash. Consequently they were looking to agist livestock to make some return on their investment. On the property where Alf sought agistment for his mob, the fencing was old but the owner assured him that it had been repaired so he left 450 tired young steers from his travelling mob there. He then returned up river to muster 500 replacement steers which had been left there the previous year. After nine months fattening they increased the value of his travelling mob considerably.

Four days later when he returned to check the 450 steers left on agistment to recuperate he found they had walked off through a wide gully where the fence had been washed out. Their tracks led south to 'Springvale' station, next door. The station was mustering in a week so he returned to the agistment property and stirred the owner to repair the fence. As he would be away attending the muster at 'Springvale' for a while, Alf wanted to be sure that the fat replacement steers had a reliable water supply in his absence. He told the landholder to get the watering point in order by fitting a float valve to the trough and removing the plug at the bottom of the six foot earth tank. Alf saw red when he brought the cattle into water at sunrise and found the float valve was not fitted and the plug still in the tank. It was a bitterly cold morning but the owner was unceremoniously dragged from his warm bed to dive to the bottom of the tank of icy water to remove the plug. Only half of the lost cattle were recovered at the 'Springvale' muster. With the exception of a few picked up by friendly drovers, the others were, to quote another popular term for cattle illegally slaughtered for meat, 'bogged in the black swamp'.

To round off the year's work, drovers hoped to pick up smaller mobs of fat bullocks for shorter trips, before they returned home well chequed up and ready for relaxation. Some drovers preferred to go off on city holidays where they could see more for their money but others just went to Camooweal, Dajarra or Winton. Here they had plenty of mates and were assured of a job when finances ran low. In most cases, holidays involved some fairly serious drinking and gallivanting with the fairer sex. Mind you, they didn't miss an opportunity on the road either. One pair of would-be casanovas arrived at a station a couple of days early to pick up a mob of fats and discovered two flirtatious house maids working in the homestead kitchen. Thinking they were on winners, they arranged an assignation after dark by some bushes outside the kitchen. In order to let the girls know when they had arrived, they were told to mimic the frog-faced owl's call, "mopoke". They called unsuccessfully for some time and then seeing the funny side of their situation, changed the call to "no poke". As it turned out, the stockcamp ringers had returned that night and jumped their claim. Such is life.

The age of cattle to go on the road for agistment caused some difference of opinion between the brothers. Alf reckoned, like most other station managers, that they should be two years old to walk the long distances without becoming leg weary. Instead, calves straight off their mothers were expected to walk hundreds of miles. By the time the mobs got to Urandangie, the soft youngsters were badly tired and agistment had to be sought for them. Caretaking and supervision of musters to send cattle on to markets from the agistment properties was Alf's responsibility and at one stage there were 'Eva' cattle on three or four properties. The brothers' intention to purchase a depot for fattening purposes never came to fruition because of the booming wool prices in the mid-fifties. No land came on the market to suit their programme.

The bigger properties selected fresh blood lines from Queensland and the bulls were walked out in mobs of several hundreds. A lot of these bulls brought brucellosis and tuberculosis into the northern herds, which took many years to eradicate. When some 'Eva' cattle from the Hamilton River agistment properties went for slaughter at a meatworks on the Queensland coast, five carcasses out of fifty-six were condemned because of T.B. Later, out of a mob of fifty-two old used bulls, slaughtered for the ground meat trade with America, seven carcasses were condemned. This was alarming. About the same time 900 dry cows went to slaughter and brought the unheard of sum of seventeen pounds ten shillings per head, delivered by rail. Because payment was on delivery to the rail head they never heard what percentage went down the chute, they were just glad to get the money.

The year prior to the 'Eva' cattle bringing this record price the Lands Department notified landholders of a substantial increase in land rents. The increase was based on a fifteen pounds per head store bullock value on the property. The Chambers lodged an appeal against the rise on the grounds that they had never received a price for their stock anywhere near fifteen pounds per head. Nine pounds per head was the best price received, and then only after driving stock to Winton or Longreach.

Land rents were based on taxation and there was a method in the Government's apparent madness. The big, company-owned enterprises had fattening depots in Queensland, where the tax rate was higher than in the Territory. The cattle finished off at these depots increased in value considerably. By putting a high value on the animal before it left the home property, the profit gained on agistment in Queensland was reduced. The Territory Government's low taxation enabled a more equitable share of bottom line market value. When the mob of 'Eva' dry cows brought such a good price the brothers were forced to drop their appeal and the following year they received twenty pounds per head for a turn off of 1,300 steers delivered to Mt. Isa.

When the fencing of the northern side of the stockroute, which passed through 'Eva', was completed, it created a secure, large, well-watered paddock which was made available for cattle agistment. The Queensland border country was in drought and the owners of 'Avon Downs', Peel River Land and Mineral Company, were seeking agistment for breeding cows. After inspecting the country and finding it suitable, the company sent off four travelling mobs, each with 1,300 head of cows and calves. The cattle came from an area of few cattle ticks into hotter country where ticks were prevalent and the owners failed to vaccinate the cattle against tick fever. Understandably, during the six months the cattle were on 'Eva', there were outbreaks of tick fever which resulted in hefty losses.

When mustered, the mob was found to be 600 head short, and a ride over the paddock revealed numerous carcasses. A rumour spread that the drover's numbers in the second and third mobs were short when they got to 'Eva', so to make up their numbers, they rode ahead in the moonlight and brought back cattle from the mob previously delivered. For a while there was suspicion that some of the cattle had been stolen but that was unlikely as they were all branded. In the end it was accepted that what cattle hadn't died of tick fever had been double-counted in the first place.

In 1957 when the water started to dry up in the flood-out country, the cattle had to be shifted to the bores and dams on the open downs. The mob included a large number of big calves that had missed being branded. Alf, who was caretaking on his own, went to Mt. Isa to employ a team of men for this job. Station hands were in short supply because the mines were paying good money. He found two young chaps who had done a little stock work and another who claimed to be a capable stockcamp cook. A third ringer was employed who claimed that he had done the lot as a station hand. When asked just what this had entailed, he replied, 'Milkin', killin' and rabbitin'.' In desperation Alf gave him a trial. This ringer told the others that he only came up north from Sydney to wear his old clothes out. It took a few days to get much work out of him because he sat firmer on a toilet seat than in a saddle. In spite of having such a patchy team, in a week the cattle were shifted and 1,230 calves were branded. The two better ringers did a great job.

One year Bruce Simpson, who helped out during the drought with boring and fencing, was the drover in charge of the 'Eva' cattle. He was so good that Alf didn't have to take the tail end of his mob for agistment at Boulia. However, a disagreement with the selling agents and a six week delay on railway trucks meant a spell had to be taken somewhere. Bruce said that at the risk of being fined he could fill in the time on the stockroute between Winton and Longreach, so Alf agreed to pay any fines incurred. Their problems were not over, however, as the first bore they came to had no water, so they had to put in ten days on the Winton common while the Shire corrected the problem. Before attempting the next dry stage of fifty-five miles, they waited a couple of days for cooler weather, gave the cattle a good, long drink and set out. On the second dry day the cattle wanted to walk for water so they were kept going into the moonlight and pulled up to camp a few miles from the bore. Next morning, Bruce, who was shorthanded, had trouble steadying the lead of the thirsty mob and Alf, who had followed in his car, helped cut the cattle into small mobs to go into the trough. Bruce kept the mob there for three weeks before proceeding to Longreach. On completion of the drive he was only down three head, all natural losses and no fines were incurred. The trip took six months and a bonus was paid for a delivery number of ninety-seven percent or better over a 1,000 miles or more. Bruce deserved every penny.

This was Bruce's swan song as a drover. He went into business as a saddler in Winton, married and became involved with community affairs. He went on to be a manager and later a director for the State Government Insurance Company (Suncorp). Bruce played a prominent part in setting up the historical museum in Winton and became a staunch supporter of the Longreach Stockman's Hall of Fame. He was also included as an ambassador for the Hall of Fame on an American tour by Australian singers, poets and songwriters. While working on 'Eva', he wrote several poems about his experiences. Bruce made a simple comment about his life as a drover. "I came out into this country many years ago with my swag which only had one blanket in it. Today, I leave with the swag cover minus the blanket."

16.

Sundown at Eva Downs

Sid continued to work between 'Eva' and Mungallala until the mid-fifties when he returned to Queensland for good. The old chap was seventy-seven, but still considered himself too young to retire. He refused to travel in a plane and instead offered his services to drover Clarrie Pankhurst who was passing through 'Eva' with a mob for Queensland. Clarrie was shorthanded and glad to take Sid along with him. With his prized kneepad saddle, swag and a port full of clothes he set out on the droving trip. At Mt. Isa he left Clarrie and took a passenger train home to Lucy's farm. Not content to be idle, after a short rest he borrowed some team horses that were no longer in use and busied himself repairing, de-silting and enlarging farm dams.

Some 8,000 acre ballot blocks came up for development in the Glenmorgan area and the old chap went to Rex Marshall, a stock and station agent in Mitchell, wishing to enter the ballot. The agent told Sid he was not eligible to make an application because of his age. "But damn it Rex, haven't I proved time and time again that I can develop virgin land." Rex certainly admired his courage!

In 1956, after collecting cattle from the agistment property on the Hamilton River and delivering them to Butru to be railed to the meatworks, Alf returned to Mt. Isa. Here the local news gave him a hell of a shock. Jack and Colin had both been charged with assaulting Aboriginal employees. Also accused was a young drover and their newly appointed manager Jack Britt, who had just arrived on the property.

The charge, assault causing grievous bodily harm, was very serious. For some time Jack had been trying to talk his two brothers into putting a manager on 'Eva' and them becoming absentee landlords. Alf and Colin disagreed and felt that at least one of the brothers should oversee the running of the property. Despite this Jack went ahead and employed a manager and a team of Aboriginal workers and their families.

Before long, Jack had a row with the Aborigines and they walked off. Shortly afterwards Jack, Jack Britt and a passing stockman were out mustering horses when the group of Aborigines jumped out of the long grass and came at the riders in a threatening manner. Jack used his stockwhip and marked one of the Aborigines and when Colin was attacked by one, he knocked him out. The stockman, who had an unregistered revolver and thinking that they were in genuine danger, fired some warning shots, which made matters worse. It was a most unnecessary and unpleasant incident for all concerned and certainly didn't help the growing tensions between the partners.

Jack had been a sickly child and was always small for his age. He liked to rule the roost and couldn't help interfering in almost everything. Instead of trying to restrain Jack's attempts to dominate the rest of the family, Sid always seemed to encourage it, often saying, "Jackie is going to be a great boss of men one day, though he will have to learn to fight."

Prior to an incident in the mid-forties, Sid had never raised a hand to any of the boys. The men were batching and Sid was doing the cooking, when Jack came in and started telling him his job. Sid flew into a rage and raised his clenched fist at Jack and chased him from the room shouting, "I've had sixty-five years experience compared to your few months, so don't you try to tell me boy!"

When Alf heard the details of the affair in Mt. Isa, he was anxious to get home but he had been having attacks of abdominal pain. The doctor didn't find any serious problems and attributed the pain to the allergy condition which often affected Alf's health. Thinking all was well, he set out for 'Eva', but by the time he arrived he was doubled up with pain. Dulcie put him to bed and nursed him along with Colin who had his leg in plaster. A young mare he was riding had bucked over and broken the foot in seven places.

Alf's pain didn't subside and Dulcie reported it to the Alice Springs Flying Doctor Base. As no plane was available, the doctor advised her to take him to Tennant Creek immediately. It was a harrowing trip for the patient who then had to travel on to Alice Springs by ambulance. Once there, he was put under the care of a wonderful Irish surgeon, Dr. Hayes, who didn't appear to be any healthier than Alf. Immediate operation was out of the question because of a high temperature which required a week of intensive treatment with intravenous antibiotics.

After a week Dr. Hayes decided Alf's condition was stable enough to operate. He was a brilliant surgeon but a very sick man, who periodically had to leave the operating table to gasp for air. The operation took four hours and revealed a ruptured appendix and peritonitis. This was once a deadly combination before the discovery of antibiotics. In the post-operative ward Alf was expertly nursed by Sister Shirley Begley. The following morning Dr. Hayes, looking very frail and drawn, examined him and said in his rich Irish brogue, "There is no doubt about it, man, ye have the constitution of a hoss!" Twenty-four hours later the good doctor died of lung cancer.

Alf's troubles were far from over. He developed post-operative complications and because there was no longer a surgeon in Alice Springs he was flown to

Darwin. In all, he was laid up for seven weeks. While he was hospitalised in Darwin, his brothers were tried on the assault charge. After a costly and damaging lawsuit both were sentenced to six months in gaol, Colin to light duties because of his broken leg, and Jack to hard labour. Jack Britt was acquitted and he was free to return to 'Eva', where with the three brothers otherwise occupied, he was sorely needed. The stockman was banned from employing Aborigines for a period of six months.

While Alf was still in Darwin, a melanoma on his lip, which had been treated previously, flared up and needed urgent specialist attention. When discharged from Darwin Hospital, he flew to Brisbane where he had quite extensive and disfiguring surgery, followed by radium treatment. When the ordeal was all over, he arrived at his mother's home a shadow of his former self, having lost two and a half stone.

While Jack was in gaol, Dulcie went to stay with her mother in Victoria to await his release. When the day arrived, she was in Darwin to greet him and take him south for six months' rehabilitation. Colin went straight home and got to work with the boring plant, making a new watering point before taking over Alf's job, caring for the cattle on agistment in Queensland. While in Boulia he got a message to return to 'Eva', because Alf had a relapse and was back in hospital. This happened at the time of the Renner Springs races in which Alf had entered some horses.

Following more surgery at the Alice Springs Hospital, this time for division of adhesions, Alf flew to Melbourne for a week where he attended the radium clinic again and visited Shirley Begley. She was about to embark on a two year working holiday to Great Britain and Europe.

Back at 'Eva', Jack Britt had left and Col went out on a boring job with Bob Chambers. When Alf returned following his second operation, he found one of Jack and Colin's Fanny Bay gaol mates caretaking and cooking while the others were out on the run. Alf started doing a small fencing job near the homestead and this chap approached him and said, "Look I'm gettin' bored doin' nothin'. Could I give you a hand?" The offer was gratefully accepted and when the work was finished, they came home and showered before tea. The chap put damper and corned beef on the table and said, "That's the best I can do. You work me too hard. I'm off on the truck coming through tonight, so make out my time." All the work he had done was stand in one place playing out wire to Alf. It was obvious that his hide was cracking and he needed an excuse to go on a bender.

On Alf's second night home at 'Eva', lightning started a bushfire and in order to save the precious grass, Alf and two ringers fought the fire with wet bags. This overexertion after his recent surgery made him feel very off-colour the next day and he recalled the old saying, "You spend the first forty years of your life trying to kill yourself. After that you spend the rest of your life trying to save what is left."

During the war years Sid had a stroke of luck when Alex Potts, an itinerant saddler, came through with two packhorses plus several good thoroughbred mares. While doing saddlery repairs at the stations all over the Barkly, he at times had his mares serviced by the stations' imported ex-race horse sires, which produced some nice foals. When he came to 'Eva', Alex was terminally ill and wanted to sell his horses to a good home. One was a colt by the 'Rocklands' sire Brown Tour out of a quality black mare that had won races in Adelaide, and he wanted him left entire.

By the early fifties, the progeny of this colt were starting to make a good name for the 'Eva Downs' horses. They were sure-footed with plenty of pace and good stock-working sense which made them much sought after by drovers for night horses. At the local race meetings, occasional ones bred out of dams with a bit of racing ability were able to hold their own against progeny of the good blood lines from the bigger stations. Race meetings were huge social events held annually at 'Brunette Downs', Renner Springs and Camooweal and were very well attended.

One year near race time Alf was talking to a drover who had just taken delivery of 'Eva' cattle. The drover said to him, "Seeing as I shall be around the race track right on race time, you had better send a telegram to the old woman."

"O.K." said Alf, "What message do you wish to send."

"Tell her — repair yourself for the 'Brunette' races."

Jack was the lightweight of the family and very keen on racing. He gave it a lot of his time and had his fair share of good wins. Unfortunately his weight restricted him to the stock-horse class for jockeys ten stone and over. For bigger races he hired a jockey. The meetings were for grass-fed horses only and the animals went into a station paddock for five or six weeks prior to the race to have them all at an identical nutritional level before being taken out for race preparation one week before the event. As there were usually fifty to seventy horses it was possible to make up good fields for the two days of racing involving six or seven races each day.

The usual programme was four or five races involving jockeys, a stockman's race for riders ten stone and over using unregistered stock-horses and a race for Aboriginal stockmen where the odds called by the bookmaker were on the rider not the horse. The locals usually bet on the best rider rather than the best horse. This race created a lot of interest and the committee sought to have a tribal elder as the judge. This system had its drawbacks when once the tribal elder declared the second horse the winner. The officials tried to correct him but he produced a tote ticket from his pocket and said, "No, the other horse won. I got him here in my pocket." His decision was accepted in accordance with the rule that the judge's decision was final.

A chap called Owen Lewis, who was of marginal weight and a genuine stockman, worked at 'Eva' for a while. He was impressed by a horse called 'Tor Spa', a gelding by the station sire from a well bred mare owned by Colin. "That big lazy horse sure has staying power provided you really work on him. Take him to 'Brunette' for the longer races and I will ride him for you."

Come race time, the horse was nominated for a special one mile trophy race. He was up against the tried and true long distance grass-fed stayers in a field of seven horses. With the big punters backing the favourites, the bookmaker's odds shortened up. 'Tor Spa' was called the longest odds of all, thirty-three to one, so Alf put five pounds on him. The race was very exciting and Owen stayed with the field and brought the gelding home to win by a short head. The delighted bookmaker claimed it as his best win ever at a country race meeting. Alf had the only bet on 'Tor Spa' and after he was paid out the bookie collected 1,370 pounds. There were a lot of long-faced punters around that day.

A week or so before the races, Jack left the station to collect the horses from the paddock to prepare them for the track. At the 'Brunette' races each station had a separate camp so Jack also set this up. One year the Beebe family from neighbouring 'Ucharonidge' were guests at the 'Eva' camp. There were three girls Nita, Florrie and Pauline. Alf took a shine to Florrie and courted her for a while.

The courtship entailed regular long rides to 'Ucharonidge', for which he used his favourite good walking mare. She wasn't much good for stock work but she could sure cover the rough ground and had no trouble doing fifty miles or so on a reasonable day's ride. The mare didn't have a name but the stockmen were quick to christen her 'Old Honeymoon'. The romance was shortlived when Alf's friend Peter Shirwin came along and cut him out. Peter bought many unbroken horses from 'Eva Downs'.

At 'Brunette' the single blokes slept out and sheltered from the strong, cold winds behind an enormous windbreak. Each camp had its own camp fire and catering facilities where parties could be held at night. Over at the track dance-hall there was a kitchen and caterers. A handyman cut up the wood to keep the buckets of water on the boil for tea making and washing up and there were four or five waitresses. Each night there was dancing and on the two main nights ladies wore long gowns. One year one of the waitresses came down with measles. She had been a popular item on the dance floor, especially amongst the trainers. Several days after the races Jack came down with the measles which he passed on to his children.

A roster of duties over race time kept things running smoothly. For several years the 'Eva' mob were detailed to select killers from the 'Brunette' herd and do the butchering. Some years as many as eight carcasses were required to provide enough meat for the crowd. On the third day it was usual to have a rodeo to wind the event up.

These meetings were usually friendly occasions with very few arguments ever coming to blows. However, one year there was a very sad incident. Two 'Eva' stockmen, who had consumed a lot of beer, decided to have a spar which developed into a serious fight. When one chap was eventually knocked out, nobody was too concerned and the party went on drinking. Five minutes later, when the unconscious stockman still hadn't stirred, someone decided to make a closer investigation. Fearing the worst, they sent for Colin and when he couldn't find the man's pulse, the flying doctor was called from the dance floor and pronounced the man dead. A post mortem was performed on the body at Tennant Creek and the finding was that death had been caused by the tongue blocking the airway. The chap who delivered the fatal blow was distraught. He was formally charged with manslaughter and the court brought in a verdict of accidental death. The stockman who inflicted the fatal blow was bound over to keep the peace for twelve months.

Throughout the twenty-three years the family spent at 'Eva', dealing a few horses to passing drovers became a hobby for whoever was at home at the time. Sometimes they sold their tired horses and bought new ones. Sid always encouraged the boys to trade in horses in order to give them a good grounding for making other business deals. Occasionally a dud cheque was received but they usually came good when the drover's contract was completed. In later years, when there was sufficient fencing, one 10,000 acre paddock was used to agist drover's horses.

Once when Alf was mustering the horses in preparation for the coming season, he discovered the station sire dead. His brothers were in Mungallala and were planning to attend the Brisbane yearling sales, so he asked them to look out for a replacement for the stallion. A while later he received a telegram from Brisbane, "Purchased three colts and Dalray arriving Mt. Isa Monday." Dalray was a high stakes winner that had recently been retired so Alf was concerned that his brothers might have mortgaged the property to buy it. Fortunately, the word filly had been left out of the message! A big trailer was borrowed from 'Brunette Downs' to transport the horses back to the station. All went well until they hit the stockroute and Alf took a corner rather sharply and tipped over the trailer spilling out the horses. Concerned that the animals might be crippled or take fright and run off, he leapt from the truck and quickly caught a couple while another chap got the halters. The horses didn't appear too upset and soon began to browse around for some grass. After a while they were led to some yards on 'Alexandria'. Alf, who had never towed a trailer loaded with horses before, realised too late that he would have been better to put the horses on the truck and the load of supplies on the trailer instead of the other way around. The only casualty was the Dalray filly. She died later as a result of an ear infection thought to have been caused by a blow to the head during the accident. Alf thought she might have been the fastest of them all.

In 1957, the first race meeting was held at Renner Springs to aid the Royal Flying Doctor Service. Alf was asked to support the meeting by bringing along some horses and it was made clear that registration and affiliation with the Australian Jockey Club was in the process of going through and would all be in order by the due date. Being a worthy cause and an excuse for a break after some hard work mustering, he was pleased to accept the invitation.

Eight or nine potential gallopers, mainly station bred horses, were mustered from the spell paddock. All were Chambers brothers' horses, except one which belonged to Jack. Alf thought Jack wouldn't mind him using the horse. After all, he and Colin always held the fort without complaint, when he took time off to train the horses for race meetings. As for the jointly owned horses, Alf considered he had every right to take them along just as Jack had on many occasions to the 'Brunette Downs' race meetings. Unfortunately, Jack did object to his and the other horses being used without consulting him and this increased the tension between the brothers.

The night before the Renner Springs races Alf was taken violently ill and before daylight the men put him on a mattress on the back of the truck to transport him to Tennant Creek hospital. When they passed the horses and men camped near the race track, Alf told the men, "Do whatever you like with them." At that stage he was too ill to care. After a brief examination by the doctor at Tennant Creek he was promptly dispatched by ambulance to Alice Springs where he underwent an operation for a bowel obstruction.

Six weeks prior to the 'Brunette' races the following year, Jack attended the club meeting. There it was disclosed that some 'Eva Downs'-bred, registered race horses had been allowed to race on an unregistered race track. As the person who had entered the horses, Alf was fined by the A.J.C. for racing registered horses on an unregistered track. A further fine was imposed on every horse raced. Jack promptly paid the fine on the horses, but Alf was so furious at the injustice of being fined when he wasn't even there, that he refused to pay. The whole business was a real kick in the guts for Alf who decided he didn't want anything more to do with the sport of kings.

When Shirley had been overseas for nearly two years, Alf received a letter from England to say that she was on her way home. After an exchange of correspondence she invited him to stay at her people's dairy farm at Orbost on the Snowy River over Christmas and New Year. At the time a chap called John Hagan had been helping Alf erect windmills, so the two of them decided to share the driving as far as Melbourne. After dropping John off, Alf drove on to Orbost and a reunion with Shirley. The couple became engaged to be married.

Alf travelled from Orbost to Mungallala where he visited his parents and told them the glad tidings and there he received a letter from Shirley saying that in order to be nearer to the station, she had accepted a nursing job back at Alice Springs Hospital. Instead of driving straight back to 'Eva', Alf decided to go via Alice Springs in order to see her. When he arrived in The Alice, she had been sent on to Tennant Creek, where the hospital was short staffed, so he finally caught up with her there.

Shirley and Alf were married and they returned to live at 'Eva' in May 1959. Initially they shared the house with Jack and Dulcie, while their own was under construction. Dulcie got along well with everybody and when there was discord in the household, her kindly influence often restored harmony.

The 'Avon Downs' cattle on agistment at 'Eva' were taken off and while a second round of mustering was done to pick up any stragglers, one of the stockmen fell off a horse and broke his collar bone. Shirley bandaged him up, but she couldn't seem to cure an Aboriginal stockman, also with the mustering team. He complained of severe headaches. When Dulcie contacted the Flying Doctor Service, they seemed to think there was no need to send a plane out and recommended that if anyone was going to Tennant Creek to bring the patients in. Shirley had to have a prenatal check, so the men were taken in at the same time. Jackie, the Aboriginal stockman, repeatedly said "Somebody point bone at me."

At the hospital both men were examined and told they could go. They didn't have any swags and there was no accommodation, so Shirley insisted that they be admitted. During the night Jackie ran a temperature, so the hospital decided to keep him in for observation. Two days later he died of meningitis.

With two families living in the same house, it wasn't long before friction developed. This became even more stressful when the building of Alf and Shirley's new home was delayed. The migrant carpenter, who couldn't read the plans for the kit home, made a terrible mess of the roof structure and then deserted them. This was very disappointing for Shirley as she was three months pregnant. With the assistance of Bob Chambers and Fred, a German migrant, Alf went on with the building. Fred, who didn't have a good command of English or carpentry, picked up John Hagan's cheque book and forged his signature. He attempted to pass the cheque in Alice Springs and got a stretch in gaol for his trouble.

The couple had only been in the new house for two days when Shirley went into premature labour. She was flown to Tennant Creek, where she lost the baby. This misfortune caused her to become severely depressed. One night when Alf walked home after his vehicle broke down, he arrived at midnight and found her busily painting the interior walls of the house. He decided there and then that she shouldn't be left alone to brood and that he should involve her as much as possible in his work on the property.

A quiet little mare called Stitches was given to Shirley to ride with him, checking the 'Avon Downs' section of boundary fencing. Everyone liked riding Stitches and Shirley had already had a couple of short jaunts on her. They were going to be out on the run for a couple of days, so spare riding horses were taken and a packhorse loaded with camp gear and swags. The first day's ride was sixteen miles and they camped on the west side of Broad Creek where Shirley was keen to assist Alf repair a fence.

Darkness brought relief from the persistent bush flies but they were replaced by mosquitoes. Citronella and a smoking camp fire helped a bit but they were so voracious that it was a relief to climb into their swag beneath the cheese cloth bush net. It was really too small for two people, but quite good for togetherness. The next day was more arduous and Shirley ended up a little saddle sore. They rode twenty-two miles before lunch and came to No. 11 bore, which had not long been completed. A good camp was made under a shady tree and Shirley lay out of the flies under the bush net reading while Alf mustered a few horses and put them in a nearby yard for the night.

Next day, after checking the final section of fencing they had lunch and set out for home with the extra horses from the yard. It was extremely hot and as they rode into the strong, hot, westerly wind they noticed increasing numbers of grasshoppers flying in the same direction as themselves. The insects reached plague proportions and irritated the loose horses being driven along in front. Shirley had to bring up the rear with the packhorse and its mates while Alf galloped off in the lead to regain control of the break-away horses.

The grasshoppers were still passing the homestead the next day and must have destroyed a lot of grass. A book which dropped from their swag on the downs was found with its few remaining pages blowing in the wind a week later. The grasshoppers had made short work of it.

It was the beginning of the end, when Colin and Jack had such a serious disagreement that they came to blows. Colin was even-tempered and by far the easiest of the three brothers to work with. It was almost impossible to have an argument with him, but neverthless Jack managed it. The result was that Colin said that he couldn't work with Jack any longer.

Colin and Alf decided it would be far better for all three to sell out and go their separate ways. The serious allergy problems that Alf experienced on the downs country combined with two major operations in recent years contributed greatly to his decision to sell, but the insurmountable problem was that it was becoming increasingly difficult to work in harmony with Jack.

Post-war 'Eva Downs', under the direction of the three Chambers brothers, was developed into a profitable and well run family business. They were years of great change. When the property was sold in 1960, it had two houses, sundry sheds and yards, was fully fenced and watered and the improved herd numbered 14,000 head of branded cattle. It was sold on a walk-in, walk-out basis for the extremely good but fair price of 230,000 pounds. Sid, by then suffering from a prostate condition, was extremely disappointed when 'Eva Downs' was sold. Nevertheless, he and Lucy came up from Queensland for the sale.

When he approached his eightieth birthday, the old chap made his remaining money over to the younger members of the family and applied for the old age pension. In his opinion he had paid enough tax during his life and now it was time to get a little back. He went along to the local constable to fill out the application form. The policeman enquired what occupation he had been engaged in during the past five years. Sid replied nonchalantly, "Oh, at times I go along collecting the hen eggs for the wife."

"Is that what you do with that horse team and scoop?" queried the jovial officer.

Epilogue

Following the sale Alf and Shirley bought a new property called 'Utopia Downs' on the Dawson River, in the Taroom district of Queensland. Here they raised a fine family of four girls and truly lived happily ever after. Shirley passed away in 1997 and Alf still works the property.

Colin married Kathy in 1960 and bought a sheep property south of Mungallala. Following a major operation he sold up and went to live in Brisbane for a time before buying a small block at Woodford where he started a Braford cattle stud. When his marriage ended in divorce he sold out and went to work with Alf until he retired to Chinchilla, where he still resides. Colin has one daughter, Danielle.

Bill was an excellent horseman and could have gone a long way as a roughrider but he preferred machinery and well-boring. After leaving 'Eva', he spent some time in the RAAF until rheumatic fever rendered him unfit. He took on wheat farming on the Darling Downs at Drillham and married Lorna and had a family of two girls and four boys. Bill died in 1994.

Jack and Dulcie remained in the Territory and bought the Renner Springs Roadhouse, which they ran for many years.

Sid eventually agreed to have a prostate operation, but he left it too late. He hated hospitals and demanded to be discharged. The doctor finally agreed provided he stayed close to the Charleville Hospital. Lucy and Olive nursed him at a local boarding house which, while they were there, caught fire and was completely destroyed. The two women had great difficulty getting Sid and the children clear of the engulfing flames. Next morning the old chap said, "Much better to be at home than be burnt to death here." They took him to 'Maroona' and employed a nurse to care for him. After three days he felt better and unobserved by all took a hoe and went off burr chipping. He passed away a few nights later aged eighty-three.

After Sid's death Lucy lived in a two bedroom cottage in Mungallala and left 'Maroona" to the youngest brother, Harry. She was happy there for eight years before going into the Roma Nursing Home, where she died in 1976.